TWO NATIONS UNDER GOD

0-8054-3130-6

Published by Broadman & Holman Publishers,
Nashville, Tennessee

Dewey Decimal Classification: 956.94
Subject Heading: ISRAEL—HISTORY
    UNITED STATES—FOREIGN RELATIONS—ISRAEL
    ISRAEL—FOREIGN RELATIONS—UNITED STATES

Unless stated otherwise, Scripture quotations are taken from:
The Holman Christian Standard Bible®,
© 1999, 2000, 2002, 2003 Holman Bible Publishers.

Verses marked NIV are from the Holy Bible, New International Version,
© 1973, 1978, 1984 by International Bible Society.

1 2 3 4 5 6 7 8 9 10 08 07 06 05 04

TWO NATIONS UNDER GOD

WHY SHOULD AMERICA CARE ABOUT ISRAEL AND THE MIDDLE EAST?

TOM DOYLE

BROADMAN
&HOLMAN
PUBLISHERS

NASHVILLE, TENNESSEE

Contents

Section 1

WHY SHOULD AMERICA CARE?

Israel is the place, and the Jews are the people whom God promises to love unconditionally forever. This produces an enormous amount of tension within the region.

The nations of the world are given an opportunity to bless or curse God's chosen covenant people. Their choice decides the health of the nation and determines its destiny. Though modern Israel's existence was off to a shaky start, America made a conscious effort to bless Israel and since that time has enjoyed the promised blessing of God. This has resulted in the United States soaring to the top of the most-favored nation list in all of recorded history.

Chapter 1

Extreme Spirituality

Jerusalem:
The Spiritual Epicenter of the World

When measuring the magnitude of an earthquake's impact, the most extreme readings are generated from the focus point commonly known as the epicenter. The earth's underground jolting quickly makes its way to the surface directly overhead, and the data are then evaluated and analyzed historically and geographically. If an earthquake is large enough, its seismic waves can be measured all around the globe.

So it is also when we move from the physical arena into the spiritual arena. From time to time there are spiritual earthquakes when religions clash and new holy wars begin. Without a doubt, the spiritual epicenter of the world is found in the tiny country of Israel and, specifically, in the city of Jerusalem. Out of all the great cities across the world, God chose Jerusalem to reside in and to place His name over forever. As a result, Jerusalem sends out enormous shock waves worldwide on a regular basis. It is, and has always been, the focal point of all spiritual history throughout the ages. No city has ever received so much attention. No city ever will.

The Anchor City of the Bible

In the Scriptures, Jerusalem, the capital city of Israel, is named 881 times. The city is so exalted that there are at least seventy names for it from cover to cover. God's love relationship with Jerusalem is seen in the tender words that He often addresses her with: "My holy city," "My highest joy," "My holy mountain." Spiritual history has been cataloged here. This is where God met with humanity and one day will again. God is attached to the city forever. That's why it's called the Holy City. How does Yahweh feel about Jerusalem?

I have consecrated this temple you have built, to put My name there forever; My eyes and My heart will be there at all times. (1 Kings 9:3b)

The LORD loves the gates of Zion. (Ps. 87:2a)

For the LORD has chosen Zion; He has desired it for His home. (Ps. 132:13)

This was the city of the prophets. This was the home of the priests. Kings ruled here. Men and women of God served here. Abraham came here to sacrifice Isaac. Jesus came here to die. Jesus continues to shock the world because He didn't stay dead here. And here again, one more time, He'll show the world He's not dead.

When eternity begins, the new Jerusalem will come down from heaven adorned like a bride on her wedding day. God's beautiful eternal love for her cannot be quenched. For more than a thousand years God's home address was there at the original "clean room" called the Holy of Holies on the Temple Mount, the very heartbeat of Israel's existence.

When I first traveled to the city of God, the effect on me was like nothing I had ever experienced. The sheer spiritual intensity of the place gripped me and wouldn't let me go. *What is happening to me?* I wondered. I couldn't get the ancient walled city out of my mind. I had already done a fair amount of world traveling, but I never once dreamed of Moscow, Buenos Aires, or even our own Washington, D.C. After visiting Jerusalem, I often returned there in my dreams. Was I experiencing some kind of spiritual breakdown?

I found out that I was in good company. After all, our Savior, the disciples, and selected prophets were all prone to emotionalism while in this majestic city. Jesus wept over it. The Twelve marveled at it. The prophets made it the focal point of their scathing messages to God's disobedient people. Jesus predicted in Matthew 24 that many would proclaim to be the Messiah in the days to come. The passage points to the tribulation period, which will be a time filled with messianic impostors. How true! In verses 23–25 of the chapter, Jesus foretold of this: "If anyone tells you then, 'Look, here is the Messiah!' or, 'Over here!' do not believe it! False messiahs and false prophets will arise and perform great signs and wonders to lead astray, if possible, even the elect. Take note: I have told you in advance."

Jerusalem has experienced this phenomenon for years. Today, I'm told that at least one person a week walks into Jerusalem and proclaims to be the true Messiah. A special wing in the city's famous Hadassah Hospital has a steady stream of delusional visitors. Some claim to be Jesus, others Elijah, John the Baptist, Moses, or one of the apostles. The majority of those who experience what is now called "Jerusalem syndrome" are American Christians! Jerusalem, it seems, has special powers over people unlike any other place.

The City That Just Can't Live Up to Its Name

Jerusalem is paradoxical by nature. Its name means the "city of peace," yet rarely does it experience any. The numbers from Jerusalem are staggering! Throughout its history Jerusalem has:

- been leveled eighteen times
- been conquered thirty-seven times
- changed hands eighty-six times

International coverage of Jerusalem routinely highlights the fact that the city is the ultimate political minefield. Over the years, a river of blood has flowed out of the city, and the riverbed appears to be widening. As I write this, the day's top news story is a suicide bombing that killed twelve Israeli citizens in Jerusalem.

How long can this go on? Dr. Charles Feinberg, in the classic work *Israel at the Center of History and Revelation*, added this:

There are many voices that fill the air today, and many of them are strident as they proclaim their versions of the solution for Jerusalem's problems. The Zionist says "nationalize." He seeks by every mean to lay heavy emphasis on the need for national consciousness and united action. The confirmed Nationalist advocates to "mobilize." For him, the way to accomplish the highest good for God's people is to muster the greatest forces to make the national will known and felt in the countries of the nations of the world. The Internationalist says "fraternize." His method of operation is to make friends of all and forget all distinctions. This is the way Jerusalem can hope to solve her difficulties. In the midst of the welter and confusion of tongues, the Psalmist cries out to "agonize." Yes, he means to pray. All too many other methods have been introduced and tried for the benefit of Israel; this avenue of prayer, of intercession, needs to be tried now, and most desperately.[1]

Through the psalms of King David we would have to conclude that God is in wholehearted agreement! He even commands all who read the Bible to pray for the peace of Jerusalem. In Psalm 122:6, David prayed for the security of those who in turn pray for his beloved city of Jerusalem. In this passionate crying out to God, David called down from heaven a showering of "peace" from God for those who love her too. The Hebrew word for peace is the familiar greeting *shalom.*

Along with peace, the word also contains in it other blessings such as prosperity, welfare, and happiness. All of these words could also be interpreted in the physical sense, but certainly God has in mind the deeper spiritual fulfillment in lack of those characteristics of true shalom. God's love for Jerusalem is without question. He even blesses those who utter a prayer for her.

Whose City?

The three great religions of the world all collide in Jerusalem. Judaism, Islam, and Christianity are deeply entwined in the fabric of the Holy City. For Jews, the glory days of the nation were generated from Mount Zion in Jerusalem. Israel soared to world prominence under David and Solomon before its spiritual implosion and subsequent captivities in later years. One of the main roads in Jerusalem is called the Street of the Prophets. Jewish influence could never be extracted from the city. All of Israel's history is tethered to Jerusalem. The people and the city cannot be separated. Even in their many centuries away from Jerusalem, the hope of a return to her filled their hearts regardless of where they lived. Jews worldwide continued to have an eye on Jerusalem throughout the years.

For Christians, the church began here on Pentecost in AD 30. Although the first-century leaders were from the northern Galilee area, the dramatic events of Jesus' death, resurrection, and ascension all took place within the same general area. A short stroll today can cover all of these historic sites within minutes. The famous southern steps between the Temple Mount and the Mount of Olives are believed to be the very ones on which Jesus often taught the multitudes. Most pilgrimages give believers an opportunity to sit on the steps and read the words that He spoke in that final week of His life. The experience is moving to say the least. It's easy to see why Christians love Jerusalem so much. Some of the most significant events in Jesus' life unfolded there. From the old city, the lights of Bethlehem are clearly seen at night only six miles away. Within those six miles between cities, Jesus was born and died. Although the major part of His life was lived in northern Israel, specifically in the Galilee area, His footprints are all over the city. The Mount of Olives, which now contains the largest graveyard in the world, will one day come alive with the return of Jesus Himself.

For Muslims, the historical attachment does not track as clearly as it does with the other two monotheistic faiths: Judaism and Christianity. Since Jerusalem is not mentioned in the Koran, the only Islamic link is the supposed tying of Muhammad's horse to the stone edifice that Jewish people affectionately call the Western Wall. I realize my above statement carries little weight with the Muslim community since Jerusalem has become their ultimate battleground. When on a recent trip to the Gaza Strip, Yasser Arafat issued a call for a million martyrs in Jerusalem. Unfortunately, in the volatile Middle East, many are more than willing to answer his call.

Islamic claims to the city are fairly recent. After the Six-Day War in 1967, Arab Muslims launched a campaign that named Jerusalem as its third holiest site. Formerly, Damascus, Baghdad, Cairo, and a host of other cities were all called the third holiest sites by various Muslim groups, ranking just behind Mecca and Medina. But now, the fervor for Jerusalem among Muslim extremists is seen all over the Middle East. Murals of the Temple Mount are painted all throughout the West Bank and in surrounding Islamic regimes with the Palestinian flag flying proudly over it. For Muslims, the one goal that will bring their solidarity worldwide is the fight for Jerusalem. This will be the battle that finally unites Arabs and Muslims. The Bible tells us that the coming battle for Jerusalem will be the bloodiest ever.

It will involve many nations in the all-out fight, but as usual it will be a battle that is spiritual in nature rather than political. It is easy to see that the conflict described on the nightly news is misunderstood and severely underestimated. It is not all about land. It is all about God.

Since we Christians believe Jesus will be the ultimate Jerusalem liberator, we have left the fate of the Holy City in His hands. As Jesus taught us, we are to "turn the other cheek" and employ completely different weapons of warfare—weapons that ultimately have greater impact. We use weapons that change lives and redirect the trajectory of destinies. They are spiritual in nature. So there were no Christian suicide bombers in Israel the last time I checked! That knocks us out of the equation in the fight for Jerusalem.

But for Jews and Muslims, the battle rages. After waiting nineteen centuries to return to Jerusalem, many Jews would have no trouble giving their lives to defend their spiritual home. They have waited so long to dwell in the city again. They have suffered so much in their long history to get back inside those old city walls. This time it is for good, though they are a tiny group compared to the world's population. They are fierce in their desire to keep Jerusalem as their spiritual and political capital.

Muslims also see the taking of Jerusalem as validation of their Islamic beliefs. Some radical Muslims believe that becoming a suicide bomber and killing many innocent Israelis in the process would only bring more "honor" to their families. Jerusalem is the ultimate conquest for Islam. Since it is home to Jews now, Muslims covet it more than ever. In 2003 on May 14, Israel celebrated its fifty-fifth birthday. Protesters in Cairo marched in defiance of the historical day. One Muslim woman held a sign that summarized the statement of the day with these words: "Go to hell! Enemies Forever!" Can we really expect these deep-seated feelings to ever leave?

Whose Land?

It is true that Jews and Arabs have struggled against each other for four millennia, but the stakes became significantly higher in the last century. The reason for this is easy to see by merely looking at a world map. Before World War I the Middle East was only a chunk of land in the middle of the Turkish Ottoman Empire. Because the Turks ultimately owned it all, the fights over land were minimal. With the collapse of the Ottomans, the landscape began to go through radical surgery. Nations like Syria, Lebanon, Jordan, and Saudi Arabia were carved into existence, and land ownership became the name of the game. For centuries the same land had been populated by local tribes. These people groups were a throwback to biblical days not only in their dress but also in their nomadic lifestyle.

All of a sudden, countries began springing to life in the 1930s and the 1940s, and national identities emerged as the area was recreated.

What about the Jews?

The Jews' desire to return to their biblical heartland was not a recent one. For centuries Jewish families dreamed of a return to their home that the prophet Ezekiel detailed in his famous "dry bones" prophecy of chapter 37. God had promised that He would gather the Jews from all the countries where they had been scattered and bring them back to their land for good. Despite the Jewish turning away from God and being displaced in the first place, these spiritual refugees would return in order that God's holy name would be exalted.

The process would be a two-step one. Old Testament Ezekiel told us in 36:24–25, "For I will take you from the nations and gather you from all the countries, and will bring you into your own land. I will also sprinkle clean water on you, and you will be clean. I will cleanse you from all your impurities and all your idols." First, Jewish immigrants would return to Israel from the four corners of the earth. Though this seemed improbable even sixty years ago, how quickly God moves when He seeks to fulfill His ancient promises. One former professor of mine, known for his particular interest and expertise in the area of prophecy, once said this: "Not all too long ago, it was laughable to most people when I talked about the enormous impact Israel would have on the world in the days to come." After all, before the Jews reinhabited it, Palestine was a barren strip of land that nobody wanted. What exactly would draw all of the nations of the world to it with their armies in the future? Today, nobody questions how important Israel is to the world's overall stability.

Israel did return to the land, and the results of this miracle are seen each and every day. The first step is completed—Israel is Israel again with a strong Jewish population right in the midst of strong regional hostility. The country's very existence forces the rest of the world to watch its every move. The first step in the miracle is "the return."

The second step of God's returning His covenant people to the land they love is "the cleansing." Israel is fragmented in its religious pursuits and for the most part quite secular. Orthodox Jews wearing side curls and Eastern European garb are what most people picture when they think of what a Jew from Israel looks like. But Orthodox Jews in Israel are only about 18 to 20 percent of the population. The rest are fairly modern and seem no different from the typical American— perhaps somewhat religious but certainly not to the degree of the bobbing Orthodox rabbis deep in prayer in front of the Wailing Wall on a daily basis.

In short, Israel does not seem a whole lot more spiritual than most other nations. In the future, as we will see throughout *Two Nations under God*, a future cleansing time of repentance is still in store for Israel—a time that will restore the people of

Yahweh to Yahweh Himself. Like returning to the land, cleansing seems unlikely. Yet, when God moves to fulfill His promises, what seems unlikely in an instant becomes reality.

The birthplace of the return appeared unlikely too. As the smoke cleared from the Nazi death camp ovens, Jewish people began immigrating both legally and illegally back to what was then called Palestine. The British blocked much of it, and as a result, Jewish organizations like the Haganah, Palmach, and Mossad were born. Members risked their lives to transfer Jews making *aliyah* (immigration) to the land of their forefathers Abraham, Isaac, and Jacob. The Jews would not be stopped. Former Prime Minister Golda Meir wrote,

> When the war ended, when Jewish lives were no longer threatened with annihilation, the Mossad continued to operate and grow not because of the rules of inertia, but because the opportunity to fulfill its ultimate task was finally at hand. From 1945 to 1948, the Mossad continued to display the same determination that characterized it during the war. It exploited every device, every trick of wit, every possible channel to defy the British blockade against Jewish immigration to Palestine and bring the Jews out of the wreck of Europe to their own land. . . . Survival was no longer sufficient as an aim. The struggle now was not for Jewish lives, but for Jewish souls—for the entire personality of Jewish people in the decades and centuries to come.[2]

As in biblical times, God used the holy and the unholy together for His glory. God miraculously gave the Jewish race its homeland back in May of 1948. The Jewish people gave God a supreme effort in making sure they arrived there.

In this historic event, the United States became a major player in the effort to give the Jews a home after the war. President Harry Truman originally had wanted to stay out of all the madness in the explosive Middle East. Great Britain had already tried to stabilize the region for thirty years without success. Despite all its efforts, the British mandate period from 1917 to 1948 was in the end a no-win situation for England. It appeared to be political suicide for Truman, and initially he was lukewarm concerning the fate of the Jews. But then God moved in his heart. Through a relationship with a former business partner, his viewpoint changed in an instant about a homeland for Jews.

Chaim Weizmann and Truman had been in a failed investment venture years before in Kansas City. The bank they helped launch failed miserably, yet a remarkable friendship began during those days that would ultimately lead to American support of the proposal sent to the United Nations that concerned partitioning part of Palestine for the Jews to return to. Truman was reluctant to visit with Weizmann, the chief architect of the push for Israeli statehood. Truman knew that Weizmann could only want one thing from the now most powerful man in the world. He wanted unconditional support for the Jews' return to Palestine. The small piece of land would be called Israel. Truman was right, and Weizmann pleaded with his old friend to step to the plate in this most historic hour of need for the Jews. In one meeting, Truman went from ambivalence to advocacy.

Realizing that the votes were going to come up short for Israel, President Truman strong-armed four nations to help swing the vote in favor of the Jews. Greece, Haiti, Liberia, and the Philippines all reversed their former position after Truman, several U.S. senators, and American businessmen applied economic and political pressure. In one instance, Harvey Firestone of Firestone Tires told the president of Liberia that if it voted against partition for the Jews, he would have to consider moving his rubber plant to another country, costing thousands of jobs and revenue to the country. Instantly, Liberia changed its vote in favor of the Jews!

There were finally enough votes in favor of partition. Truman had seen to it. Although our president's motives were hardly spiritual, God used all of it to magnify Himself and His ultimate purposes. Like other times in Israel's history, God used everything from a talking donkey to a bitter enemy to further His plans. God's ability to orchestrate the good, the bad, and the ugly for His desires worked once again. His moving in an American president's heart was the key to setting it all in motion. Harry Truman became a powerful instrument in the mighty hand of God.

With enormous tension in the air, United Nations delegates flooded into the assembly hall November 29, 1947, in Flushing Meadow, New York, to decide the future of God's chosen people. Had He completely forgotten them? After all, with normal annual population growth rates, the Jews should have totaled about 120 to 140 million worldwide. With barely 12 million left on the face of the earth, Yahweh remembered His covenant people once more! The entire gathering of politicians, reporters, and spectators was now set, and the auditorium fell silent. As the delegate from Guatemala rose to cast the first vote, a cry from a lone voice in the audience summarized Jewish feelings worldwide. In Hebrew, the words that filled the room were "Oh Lord, save us!" Within a short while, after tallying the votes, the short prayer that contained all of history was answered yes by God. Israel would indeed return, not to Palestine but to Israel. As a young boy, my uncle told me that the greatest event in the twentieth century was not that the Allies defeated Nazi Germany and avoided world takeover. But rather, that God answered the aching prayer from Jewish hearts worldwide to return to their homeland after so many years.

On the same day the votes were cast, another miracle happened that was not coincidental. This one occurred far from New York, back in the biblical city of Jesus and King David in Bethlehem. While the votes were being read on the live radio broadcast around the world, Hebrew University professor Eleazar Sukenik took a six-mile bus ride from Jerusalem and bought the first installment of the famous Dead Sea Scrolls from Kando, the Arab broker of the precious parchments. Having been warned that if partition was approved his life would certainly be in danger in the mostly Arab village, Professor Sukenik ignored the advice and made the journey anyway. As all in Jerusalem were listening to the final vote being read, Eleazar opened the first scroll and read God's eternal Word from the prophet Isaiah that predicted the Jewish return centuries before. In one miraculous day, Israel had its beloved land back, its sacred Scriptures back, and the reassurance God had indeed not forgotten them.

Home at Last!

Israel had truly experienced a miraculous rebirth. Not one nation's people in history had ever come close to returning to their former homeland after a nineteen-hundred-year absence. The Jews had never fully assimilated into the more than one hundred nations where they had been scattered. Their return to the land was always in some sense the fuel that kept the flame of their existence flickering. Now they were home. Their rebirth once considered impossible became possible.

The Hebrew language was also revived. The language had not been spoken for about twenty-five hundred years. Ever since Israel's Babylonian captivity, the language of the people had ceased being Hebrew. Rabbis and scholars knew the ancient tongue, but the common folk soon adopted Aramaic and Greek, and soon the Hebrew language became a dead one. Even in Jesus' day the people spoke Greek, and as a result it became the language of the New Testament. Again the God of the Hebrews made good on an ancient promise. In the book written by the minor prophet Zephaniah in about 640 BC, God had again promised something that appeared highly unlikely. He said this in 3:9: "For I will then restore pure speech to the peoples so that all of them may call on the name of Yahweh and serve Him with a single purpose." What would this language be? Hebrew, of course! The ancient tongue of God's people. How could the dead language come to life again? Eliezer Ben-Yehuda was the philologist who spent the majority of his days bringing the language back to life, making it modern and spoken again. Remarkably, Ben-Yehuda had to invent Hebrew words to match ordinary words that had come into being over the twenty-five centuries of Hebrew disuse. Words like "United States," "outer space," and "pizza" had to be formed in Hebrew. Eliezer used parts of Hebrew words to come up with the whole new vocabulary. He spent about fifty years of his life in this task. Never once in history had a dead language been revived. It could only happen to the people whose God had chosen them and had performed the impossible over and over throughout their entire existence. To Bible readers, after all of this happened overnight, the turnaround was like a modern-day exodus from Egypt.

Not everyone, however, was thrilled. David Ben-Gurion, Israel's first prime minister, announced on May 14, 1948, that Israel was officially a nation again. On May 15, five Arab nations attacked the one-day-old country. The Jews' zeal to return to their ancient land was greeted with outright rejection by their neighbors. Even today, many Arabs call the birth of Israel the *nackba*—the tragedy. Since the nation's inception it has experienced a major war every decade, and it looks as if another one may start soon. Yet Israel still perseveres through adversity. To emigrate from the United States or any other part of the world to Israel is not only admirable but certainly high risk. But Jews keep coming because no war, no strife, no threats can extinguish the flame in the heart of every Jew for their beloved Israel.

Islamic threats to Israel's existence are on the rise now that Osama bin Laden, Saddam Hussein, and even Yasser Arafat have risen to heroic proportions. In West Bank towns and in the Gaza Strip, young people now trade "martyr cards" that look exactly like American baseball cards and are prized by collectors. Muslims, it seems, have seized a Christian term for saints of God who die for their faith and have applied it to their terrorists who commit murder and suicide at the same time. A *shaheed* brings honor to their family. When Saddam Hussein was in power, he personally sent each suicide bomber's family a $25,000 check. Samuel Smadja, who has lived his whole life in Jerusalem, often quotes former Israeli Prime Minister Golda Meir who when asked when there will be peace in Israel said, "When they love their children more than they hate us."

The Goal—Jerusalem

When all is said and done, the reason for the battle is, of course, for the ultimate prize—Jerusalem. In short, the spiritual epicenter of the world will always be right in the middle of a major fault line. Earthquakes will continue to reverberate from the Holy City of God until Jesus returns and creates one of His own. As Christians we have a permanent connection to Jerusalem. Our spiritual roots are buried deeply in Holy Land soil. We are grafted into Israel as Romans 11 tells us. Roughly 85 percent of Scripture is about Israel. Our Messiah was Jewish, and so were the first church leaders. The prophets were Jewish. In addition, sixty-four of the sixty-six books of the Bible were Jewish authored. Luke was the only Gentile author of Scripture, penning under the inspiration of the Holy Spirit the Gospel of Luke and the Acts of the Apostles.

The kingdom of the future millennium will be established, of course, in Jerusalem, Israel. So, how can we just sit by and watch this systematic unraveling of our spiritual capital city?

True, the fate of the Holy City is in our Savior's powerful, loving hands, yet we can still be involved. What role does America play in all this? What role does the church play? Can we still make a difference? We can, and we should! The following chapters will help you see how.

★ ☼ ★ ☼

Avi—The Reconciler

AVI HAD ALWAYS APPRECIATED his Jewish roots. Born into a more traditional Israeli family in Tel Aviv, he always observed the Jewish holidays. Avi was the typical young Jewish Israeli with dreams of exploring the world to see what it had to offer. He especially had a desire to visit Las Vegas, Nevada, to get rich.

At one point in Avi's life, his sister shared with him her newfound faith in Yeshua (Jesus). Avi had no interest in religion at that time and did not seriously consider his sister's comments. Upon visiting her later in Florida, he was somewhat confused about why his Jewish sister would be attending a Baptist church. Out of curiosity, he decided to attend this church at his sister's invitation. He was shocked at what he observed and encountered there. Immediately, he was struck by the passionate worship as he entered the sanctuary. His shock turned to amazement as he realized the people, many of whom were Gentiles, were more familiar with the Scriptures than he was as a Jew. He noticed a profound joy that filled the people's hearts. This provoked his heart to jealousy for what they had.

Avi was about to experience the ultimate paradigm shift. *How could all of this be real?* he thought. Yet the joy in the room awaited to fill his heart, and deep down inside he longed to be filled with this kind of joy. In Romans 11:11, Paul said that "salvation has come to the Gentiles to make Israel jealous."

This is what was happening in Avi's heart! He asked himself, *Why do they have such joy? Could these people possibly possess what I have always longed for . . . a living relationship with God?* After hearing the gospel taught at a youth group, Avi reached out to his Jewish Messiah in childlike faith. His loving Father reached out to him as Avi received Jesus, the Jewish Messiah, as his Savior, and immediately an inner joy he had never known flooded his soul. He now has the living relationship with God that he desired.

Today, Avi lives near Tel Aviv and reaches people of all races and religions for Messiah Yeshua through the Dugit Messianic Outreach Center (*dugit* means "small fishing boat" in Hebrew) right off Dizengoff Square in the heart of the city. He has a passion to see Jews and Arabs come to know Yeshua and be reconciled together as the "one new man." Avi has a godly wife, Chaya, and three daughters and also pastors the Adonai Roi Messianic Congregation in Tel Aviv (*Adonai Roi* is Hebrew for "the Lord is my Shepherd"). This dynamic congregation works hand in hand with the Dugit Messianic Center to reach the lost with the gospel and disciple them as believers in their Jewish Messiah Yeshua. It has a steady stream of new believers as a result of its sensitive, yet powerful, outreach efforts in which teams come from all over the world to help share the gospel of Yeshua. Russian Jews, Orthodox Jews, Palestinian Arabs, and an assortment of agnostics, atheists, and New Age followers have been rescued from the kingdom of darkness at Dugit.

Among believers, Avi is a respected and recognized leader in Israel. His congregation has multiplied and sent others to plant new congregations. He also works with other ministries. Currently, Avi and his leadership team are praying about beginning another outreach center, "Dugit 2." The God of Abraham, Isaac, and Jacob made Avi jealous through the Gentiles before He made him zealous for Him and the lost sheep of Israel. Avi is a true hero in Israel, yet he constantly battles persecution, threats, and discrimination from some of the religious Jews and antimissionary organizations. The bulk of the persecution comes from the Orthodox Jewish leadership. During street preaching, it's not uncommon for local religious Jews to shout, blow whistles, and scream at Avi during his messages. With patience and a big smile, his gentle answer turns away their wrath, and the joy he displays gets the attention of skeptics who also hunger as Avi once did. Avi speaks the truth straightforwardly, and the people drink it in. Yeshua's words in John's Gospel are also fitting of Avi: "Here is an Israelite in whom there is nothing false."

★ ✡ ★ ✡

So that He might create in Himself one new man from the two, resulting in peace. [He did this so] that He might reconcile both to God in one body through the cross.
EPHESIANS 2:15b–16a

Chapter 2

Endangered Species

*Twenty-three nations throughout history have made the
fatal mistake of cursing Israel by their words and actions
and have paid the ultimate price—extinction. Is God's promise
"to curse those who curse" Israel still valid today?*

Forever Is a Long Time

Throughout the scope of human history, certain themes emerge
consistently from generation to generation. These themes are
often simple in nature. Here are a few:

- Empires come and empires go.
- Good rulers and evil rulers become powerful and then
  fall.
- Nations rise to prominence only to fall backward into
  mediocrity.

At times, people groups and leaders appear invincible, yet
time and mortality eventually level the playing field, and their
greatness fades.

In his excellent work *Israel and the Nations*, F. F. Bruce
explained Israel's remarkable stature among the Middle East
nations: "Israel's national history was not lived out in isolation
from other peoples. The Israelites were surrounded by nations
greater and mightier than themselves, who impinged upon the
life of Israel at innumerable points. It is in the varied response to
the challenge presented by these other nations, Asian, African,
and European, that Israelis' own nationhood acquires its special
character."[1] Bruce's point is well taken. The uniqueness of the

nation of Israel is found in the fact that it is as relevant to the world's overall stability today as it was in Old Testament times. Bruce went on to say,

What (is) so special about this one small nation of antiquity? Why should the story of Israel still be of interest and relevance to us in the late twentieth century and beyond? The answer to these questions can be found nowhere but in the distinctive features of Israel's religion. There was something about it that was unparalleled in the surrounding world. An Assyrian king once tried to discourage any resistance on the part of the Israelites by pointing to the uselessness of the gods of greater and more powerful states, which he had overthrown. "Where are the gods of Hamath and Arpad?" (2 Kings 18:34), he asked. A question which might well be repeated today. Where indeed are they? And how does it come about that the God of Israel continues to be worshipped by millions of people in every one of the earth's continents? The Israelites had their own explanation. As they considered their experience of the God of their fathers, they affirmed, "He has done this for no other nation" (Psalm 147:20). Their affirmation is vindicated by the course of their history.[2]

In biblical days, several nations living in Israel's backyard periodically exhibited as much swagger as an NBA superstar. Yet their pride ran its course, and soon they also lay among the fallen. Israel, however, remained. In some cases, these nations paid the ultimate price for their arrogance—extinction. They were wiped off world maps forever. Why is it that twenty-three different nations, mentioned in the Bible and once vibrant and powerful, no longer exist today? In the animal kingdom, species come and go throughout time. There is the endangered species list that garners the world's attention as another animal group tiptoes toward oblivion. Worldwide efforts are launched to save the shrinking population of a species, and when carried out far enough in advance, the animals survive. There are failures, many of them. Gone is the giant skink. The Cuban macaw will never return, no matter how much it is missed. The T. rex likewise was erased from existence centuries before our lifetime, thankfully. When we move from animal groups to people groups, just what was it that these nations did to appear on the Bible's endangered species list? No matter how hard they tried, they eventually died out altogether.

First Things First

In Psalm 47:2, the sons of Korah remind us that God is the "great King over all the earth." From His holy throne, He reigns over the nations and owns the kings of the earth. The sons of Korah knew this all too well. It was their family that rebelled against Moses and Aaron in the desert and faced an immediate execution when God sent an earthquake from below and fire from above to squelch their little protest. To say the least, Korah and his 250-man opposition group were dealt with in seconds. God allowed a few of the descendants to survive, and for centuries their very presence among the Israelites made the people think long and hard before they opposed God or His current leader. God's zero-tolerance stance on rebellion would travel outside of His holy nation and soon afflict several of the unholy nations. God's endangered species list would grow and grow quickly. Yet, other times, nations like Egypt rebelled against God and survived. Was God being unfair?

A Promise Is a Promise

In the first book of the Bible, God called a man from a pagan land and a pagan family; His opening promise to him spelled out clearly the formula for the future survival of all nations. He promised Abram to:

- make him into a great nation
- bless him
- make his name great
- bless those who blessed him
- curse those who cursed him
- bless all peoples through him

The promise that turned Abram into Abraham began a chain of events resulting in the birth of the nation of Israel and eventually the birth of the Messiah Himself. The entire world would be blessed by the coming Savior through Abraham's line. The entire world would be given the opportunity to bless or curse Abraham's line. God set it in stone. He repeated it several times. He then gave each nation the chance to "weigh in" in regard to the promise. Amazingly, the promise given in Genesis 12 was exactly a chapter after the one in which God Himself scattered the nations of the world from the Tower of Babel. The die was cast. National survival was at stake. Many nations opposed Israel throughout their history, but the ones that outright cursed God's nation authored their own personal death sentence.

Anyone Seen a Hittite Lately?

The list is long, hard hitting, and comprehensive. The roll call of the annihilated has a familiar ring to it. Like an issue of "whatever happened to . . ." from *People* magazine, the names are familiar; and their final days, when compared, are all similar. The Hebrew word for curse, *haram*, means "to seclude from society." Therefore, when nations cursed Israel, they selected the Hebrews from society to be the focal point of their hatred. They singled them out from all others and fervently worked to destroy them. Since God chose Israel and determined to lavish the Hebrews with His love and His direct involvement, He had no choice but "to seclude from society" that particular nation and destroy them. In short, if a nation cursed Israel, God then cursed that nation. There would be no "fudging" with God. Not three strikes but one. Kingdoms and rulers would rise and fall. Israel would cycle through times of faithfulness and times of utter paganism. It didn't matter. God continued to keep score—the Hittites, the Jebusites, the Perrizites, and the Ammonites.

Empires came and went. Leaders rose and fell. Nations ruled vast empires and then suddenly weren't major players anymore. God simply hit the delete key, and they were gone. Several of God's leaders witnessed this phenomenon while serving as shepherds over Israel. Abraham, Moses, Joshua, the judges, and David all stood against mighty forces that were suddenly gone and never a threat to them again. Like a great row of dominoes, each one fell rather quickly—their cities and territories taken over by other civilizations and ruins built upon ruins. In some cases, the Bible was the only record of their existence. Later on, as archaeological mound sites called tels in Israel were excavated one by one, layers of history were peeled back. Archaeologists rediscovered lost people groups that had been so thoroughly destroyed that at one point Bible skeptics doubted they had ever truly existed at all. The footprints of their existence were unmistakable. The people, however, had disappeared centuries ago—the Canaanites, the Amorites, the Hittites, the Amalekites.

> Do not fear, you worm Jacob, you men of Israel: I will help you—the LORD's declaration. Your Redeemer is the Holy One of Israel. (Isa. 41:14)

> Remember, LORD, [what] the Edomites said that day at Jerusalem: "Destroy it! Destroy it down to its foundations!" Daughter Babylon, doomed to destruction, happy is the one who pays you back what you have done to us. (Ps. 137:7–8)

In that day—the LORD's declaration—will I not elim-
inate the wise ones of Edom and those who understand from the hill country of Esau? Teman, your warriors will be terrified so that everyone from the hill
country of Esau will be destroyed by slaughter. You
will be covered with shame and destroyed forever
because of violence done to your brother Jacob.
(Obad. 8–10)

In the New Testament, the church is called to go to the
nations where God's precious grace can be offered to each of
them. In the Old Testament, Israel was to influence the nations
of the world also. What influence it wielded! The people of Edom
were not the only people whose "forever" was radically changed.

Don't Mess with Israel

Striking out at God's chosen people was one thing. Cursing
and calling for their destruction was another. When a nation
went that far, God was sure to act. The words you see were
more than slander; they were an attack on God Himself. In his
book *Israel the Land and the People*, Wayne House correctly
summed it all up with these words: "But the land of Israel is not
just dirt and rock. It is more than mountain and plain. The land
of Israel is a promise of God. It is a promise so strongly held by
Him that He stakes His promise concerning the land to His eternal character."[3] If God is this zealous for His land, imagine how
much He cares for the people who live in it. In the future, the
two will be united under the divine rule of God. House continued: "The land of Israel is where the people of God will enjoy
the presence of God under the reign of God in the Kingdom of
God. Ultimately, the land of Israel is the center of the planet,
the focal point of the universe—for the outworking of the purposes of God Eretz Israel! The land of Israel is the enduring

physical place for the outworking of God's plan."[4] The nations of the world would tread on holy ground when they entered the borders of Israel. They would be allowed to walk on the land but never to walk on God's people. Listen to God as He speaks of His beloved people Israel: "For the LORD's portion is his people, Jacob his allotted inheritance. In a desert he found him, in a barren and howling waste. He shielded him and cared for him; he guarded him as the apple of his eye" (Deut. 32:9–10 NIV). Five phrases in the passage vividly detail God's feelings about His chosen nation:

"The LORD's portion"

The picture is one of food as God says Israel is all He needs to be satisfied. Later in Psalm 119:57, the writer said, "The LORD is my portion." How beautiful it is to see God and His people wholly satisfied with each other. Like a dinner plate artistically arranged with the most delicious meal imaginable, God says Israel is all He needs to be filled up and content. He expects us to feel the same way about Him, as the psalmist did.

"His allotted inheritance"

In biblical days, every family of Israel except the Levites had an inheritance in the land. These precious parcels of land were handed down through the generations and never traded or sold. The inheritance was each family's identity. When asked where an Israelite was from, his answer also revealed who his family was. In short, an inheritance of land told where he lived and who he was. God linked Himself to Israel by defining where He would live and who He would call family. No other nation but Israel enjoyed this high privilege of living with God and being called His own.

"He shielded him"

If there was one thing Israel knew about, it was war. In the Israelites' history, they rarely experienced anything else. Even today, since becoming a nation in 1948, Israel has experienced six major wars and several conflicts. With the Gulf War, the intifada, and the constant barrage of terrorism, Israel can never rest. If God had not been shielding the Jews continually, they would have ceased to exist centuries ago. Frederick the Great once demanded an answer of one of his servants concerning the veracity of the Scriptures. He asked, "Why should I believe the Bible?" His servant replied, "I can answer that in one word . . . *Israel.*" Apart from God, there is no reason for Israel's continued existence. This is a people group that keeps coming back when given up for dead. Its survival depends on God's shield—daily.

"And cared for him"

With all its wars, captivities, anti-Semitic attacks, and attempted systematic killings called "pogroms," Israel has been bruised and bloodied for much of its existence. Shepherds have always roamed the Judean hills, and their firm, loving care for their sheep is an ongoing reminder of their Father's care for them. Throughout the years, the Jews had God alone to care for them. More often than not, they have been at odds with the majority of nations. Today is no different. Even though presently they remain largely secular, there is a frequent SOS to God that goes out collectively from these battered and bruised people. God always answers their cry. He always will. He has shepherded them over forty centuries.

"The apple of his eye"

This phrase may explain more about the phenomenon of Israel's continued existence than any other words in Scripture.

Three times God calls Israel the apple of His eye. Since the apple refers to the pupil, four things are learned about God's personal connection to Israel:

1. It is easily injured. A mere eyelash when stuck on the pupil can bring instant pain that demands one's attention, pronto. God says every injury to His people is an injury to Him, and His pain is never unnoticed.

2. It cannot be repaired. Once the pupil is damaged, there is no medical procedure to repair it. Over the centuries, nations have brutally attacked Israel. Egypt, Babylon, and Rome all did, and God experienced pain over each act of violence. They would be dealt with in the future.

3. It gives direction. Israel was to be God's leader among the nations. The Jews' lives and their relationships with God were to be a light for the Gentiles to follow to God. Isaiah thundered, "'You are my witnesses,' declares the Lord!" (NIV). Israel was to be the eyes for all the nations in darkness—sight for the helpless, direction for the lost.

4. It is protected. As natural as it is for us to deflect anything headed for our eyes, so it is with God. He protects Israel as if He were protecting Himself. It's reflexive, natural, and done quickly. "For this is what the LORD said to me: As a lion or young lion growls over its prey when a band of shepherds is called out against it, and is not terrified by their shouting or subdued by their noise, so the LORD of Hosts will come down to fight on Mount Zion and on its hill. Like hovering birds, so the LORD of Hosts will protect Jerusalem—by protecting [it], He will rescue [it], by sparing [it], He will deliver [it]" (Isa. 31:4–5).

The tally continued: the Philistines, the Moabites, the Edomites, the Kerethites, the Pelethites, and the

Hamathites. "In the year that King Ahaz died, this oracle came: Don't rejoice, all of you [in] Philistia,
because the rod of the one who struck you is broken.
For a viper will come out of the root of a snake, and
from its egg comes a flying serpent. Then the firstborn
of the poor will be well fed, and the impoverished will
lie down in safety, but I will kill your root with hunger,
and your remnant will be slain. Wail, you gates! Cry
out, city! Tremble with fear, all Philistia! For a cloud
of dust is coming from the north, and there is no one
missing from [the invader's] ranks. What answer will
be given to the messengers from that nation? The
LORD has founded Zion, and His afflicted people find
refuge in her" (Isa. 14:28–32).

"An oracle against Moab: Ar in Moab is devastated,
destroyed in a night. Kir in Moab is devastated,
destroyed in a night. . . . For their cry echoes throughout the territory of Moab. Their wailing reaches
Eglaim; their wailing reaches Beer-elim. The waters of
Dibon are full of blood, but I will bring on Dibon even
more [than this]—a lion for those who escape from
Moab, and for the survivors in the land" (Isa. 15:1, 8–9).

Implicitly, Jews understood the enormous value of Jewish
lives. Over time, they witnessed numerous attempts to ethnically cleanse them from the planet. If God was willing to wipe
out entire people groups for their treatment of His chosen ones,
then every life was important, even if only one were at stake.

Ehud Avriel, who helped create Israel's famous underground spy network known as the Mossad, wrote in his book
Open the Gates!, "In the summer of 1944, the Soviets advanced
into Nazi-occupied Europe, and with unbelievable speed the
liberating armies reached the borders of Rumania and Bulgaria.
As they moved on, Jews in their communities and centers of
deportation carefully dared to raise their heads and look

around—the nightmare was over. Pessimists had always predicted that our rescue efforts could never save meaningful
numbers of Jews, but we in Istanbul, and most Jews in
Palestine, believed that the rescue of even a single life was to
justify the greatest efforts, expenditures, and risks."[5] Though it
was undoubtedly one of the darkest periods in Jewish life with
six million horrible deaths in Nazi concentration camps, the
price of saving even one life was entirely worth it. If God
wanted to protect His people so vigorously, then it's easy to see
why Jews put such a premium on life itself. They were not dis-
posable. There were no throw-away lives. Admittedly, after the
Holocaust, many Jews questioned whether God's desire was to
still protect them at all. Perhaps this is the most serious stumbling block in Jewish evangelism.

On a recent trip to Israel, I had the privilege of meeting a
woman who is a Holocaust survivor. She was residing in a rehabilitation center in Tel Aviv because her age and painful journey
through life had now caught up with her physically. Despite the
tragedies she had witnessed, remarkably her nature was positive, upbeat, and happy. Her parents had died in the *Shoah*
(Hebrew for Holocaust). Most of her family had also. I found
this lovely lady a blessing to speak with. Her resilience was
amazing. Life had not dealt her a bad card, and she believed
that the God of Israel was still firmly in control of things. She
even ventured to say that peace in Israel was on its way. How
delightful she was! How rare!

For so many people, their understanding of God is shaped by
their life experience. One of the most difficult tasks we have as
humans is to avoid becoming "experiential theologians," those
who derive their views of God solely from their experiences.

It is hard to fault Jews around the world who for the most
part have become practical agnostics. I dare not point a finger
at them. My ethnic group, the Irish, has not endured a fraction
of what Israel has undergone and continues to. That is why I

believe Jewish outreach must be sensitive, respectful, and loving. These are a people whose existence has been far more difficult than any other's. No one comes close. The only one that possibly could have kept them going through time and history is God Himself. He fights for them. Always has. Always will. Many a Jew will say, "Where was God during the Holocaust?" One Jewish man from Tel Aviv remarked to me recently, "I thank God we are His chosen people. I just wish He would choose someone else for awhile." Most certainly God has allowed Israel's endless pain and suffering for some reason. What is it? Before you finish this chapter, you'll find out why.

Whatever Happened to Rome?

What about today? Nations appear to curse God's people and still survive. I haven't seen the fire of God. Is there some sort of plan B? For all that Nazi Germany did to the Jews of Europe, it would seem that it should be smoking ruins and nothing more. The Spanish Inquisition of the 1400s forced Jewish people to renounce their religious faith and become a *converso* or "convert" to Christianity. This was evangelism at one of its lowest moments. If Jews wouldn't convert, they were executed. Yet Spain still stands today.

Likewise, in the first century, Rome was the power broker of the world. To Rome, Israel was only an insignificant group of religious nuts who continually wasted the Romans' time and dominated their overextended military. After the Jewish revolt in AD 66, Rome had had enough. They moved into the Holy Land in full force under General Titus, and the results were disastrous for the Hebrews. The prolonged siege on Jerusalem was complete with ramparts to easily climb over the city walls and towers to shoot down at any resisters. The sacking of Jerusalem was complete. The second temple, built by Governor Jerubbabel, King David's descendant, in 520 BC and enlarged by

Herod the Great five centuries later, was destroyed. One and a half million Jews were killed by the world's most powerful army. Many were burned alive or thrown off of the city walls to their deaths. All temple treasures, utensils, and holy articles were carried off to Rome. Even the gold on the inner temple walls was confiscated after the smoke cleared. In fact, the present day Western Wall that religious Jews pray at so fervently was the retaining wall underneath the temple complex. The Romans proudly left it as a testimonial to their greatness. Their trophy was meant to point out that Rome prevailed over Israel as no other nation had.

In archaeological finds near the fallen city walls, some perplexing discoveries were unearthed. Major temple stones weighing several tons were hundreds of feet away from their obvious placements in the overall structure. The question is why the Romans would take the time to drag these monolithic heavyweights so far from the temple. Ronnie Cohen, a top tour guide in Israel, recently said that a plausible theory to explain the massive stone removals is that the Romans blew up the temple. Blew up the temple? After he explained it, it made sense. The Romans would have been foolish to waste the time and manpower to move the stones so far away. There would be no need for it either. Cohen believes General Titus's army cut down olive trees, plenty of them, from the Mount of Olives just across the Kidron Valley. Next, they placed the trees under the water channels and tunnels directly under the temple. Since the channels were filled with water, the constant burning of the trees over time caused the water to become so hot that eventually it boiled and then finally erupted, causing an explosion that sent crafted boulders to their resting places far from the temple.

However the Romans leveled the temple, they did quite a job! Arrogantly, they carried their spoils back to Europe and boasted that gods of Rome were more powerful than the God of Israel. Certainly the mighty empire would fall, but somehow one of Israel's worst enemies avoided a divine wiping out. Why them and not the Hittites? Why does Germany exist but not the Canaanites? Spaniards still reside in Spain. Why don't Edomites still dwell in Jordan?

What about the Promise to Curse Those Who Curse Israel?

Certainly a case is made for the fact that each of these nations after attacking Israel wielded considerably less influence. No one is worried about Italy becoming the next superpower and taking over the world. In its heyday, Spain became a world leader mainly through its conquests on the sea. In the tenth century, the Spaniards enjoyed a golden age of Jewish science, literature, and philosophy. Jews enjoyed more freedom in Spain than in any other European country. In some cases, they even held high offices within the government. Over the next few centuries, that would all change. By the time King Ferdinand and Queen Isabella reigned in the 1400s, Jews were openly called Marranos (swine), and the Spanish Inquisition was underway. A Jewish writer of the day penned these words, "One third of the Marranos have perished in the flames, another third wander homeless over the earth seeking where they may hide themselves, and the remainder live in perpetual terror of a trial."[6] At the height of hysteria, the king and queen gave Jews a four-month opportunity to leave or face execution. They fled to other countries like Russia, Turkey, and Eastern Europe, where later persecution continued. The location was new but the tactics were old, as over the years God's chosen people ran from one pogrom to another. Again Spain fell from its lofty position, going from superpower to also-ran, never returning to its prominence again. However, somehow it avoided the wrath of God's judgment.

Today, with six million Jews back in the biblical land of Israel, they are again in a familiar position—surrounded by their enemies! Outnumbered nearly one hundred to one, citizens of Israel are in the middle of the highest concentration of Jewish haters on the face of the earth. Islam teaches that no land under the control of Muslims can ever again be ruled by "infidels." The fact that Israel exists as a nation and not only exists but thrives in the hostile surrounding is a major embarrassment to the Muslim world. That the land once conquered and controlled by the Islamic Ottoman Empire of Turkey for four hundred years has now slipped through their hands and was lost is more than Muslim leaders can stomach. That the land was lost and is now in the hands of Jews makes it ten times worse for any Koran-believing Muslim. In some cases, Israel's existence is ignored altogether. Weather maps and geography books in many Muslim countries show the land of Israel yet fail to even put a name on the territory.

The law of diminishing influence is certainly visible in today's Muslim empire. With recent statistics from the United Nations, Islamic countries rank the lowest of the low in national literacy and abject poverty. The mighty empires of the past like Egypt continue to wallow well behind the majority of the world, all the time having to watch Israel grow and prosper. If it wasn't for their vast oil reserves, they would be as insignificant as the underdeveloped countries in Africa.

What's amazing to realize is that Arab people truly have one of the most beautiful cultures in the world. Their warmth, passion for life, and hospitality can hardly be rivaled. What's sad about Middle Eastern Arab culture is that it experienced a hostile takeover at the hands of the Muslim religion. As Jews rejected Islam and Arabs embraced it, a poisonous hatred permeated the region. Hatred of Israel came to be the unifying theme of Middle Eastern Islamic countries.

I have to say at this point, most Arabs and also most Muslims do not experience a latent desire for the state of Israel to be driven into the sea. Yet, because Islam is only compatible with governmental dictatorships, somewhat like the Mafia, the worst and the cruelest often rise to the top positions of power. One exception was Jordan. The late King Hussein, though thoroughly Muslim and a supposed descendant of Muhammad, appreciated Israel and conducted secret meetings with former Prime Minister Golda Meir.

At best, Islamic nations of the region tolerate the existence of Israel. At worst, other Islamic nations look for, pray for, and find their national identity in an outright destruction of Israel. Recently a reporter in Egypt questioned why so many Islamic nations were in financial chaos and plagued by illiteracy. He concluded that the best way to advance themselves was to give up one thing and one thing only—a hatred of Israel. He is absolutely right! Within the day that his article was published in Cairo, threats to the newspaper began immediately, calling for his death. Arab nations sadly will remain in a virtual "dark age" until the death grip of Islam is released and the true beauty of Arabs emerges again. Until then, their influence is diminished.

When God Comes Through

What do all of Israel's enemies throughout the centuries have in common? Each one of them has a coming appointment with God. It can't be rescheduled or skipped, and no one will be late. An audience with the King of Kings is going to be held in the future, and all the nations will be in attendance. The book of Joel gives us a glimpse of the Gentile judgment in chapter 3 starting in verse 1. What's so significant about this time is that the nations have not been assembled like this since their meeting on the plain of Shinar at the Tower of Babel. Because the people would not listen to God's command to fill the earth,

He forced it on them. By creating a multitude of languages, the people stumbled away in confusion, and the nations of the world began. The last meeting they called. This one God calls.

The scene takes place in the Kidron Valley just east of the Temple Mount in Jerusalem. God first "restores" the fortunes of Judah and Jerusalem. They are then firmly planted in the land with no more talk of displacing them or conquering them. Then God says to all the nations gathered in the famed Valley of Jehoshaphat, "I will enter into judgment with them there because of My people, My inheritance Israel" (Joel 3:2b). Matthew told us in chapter 25 of his Gospel that nations will be divided into two groups—sheep and goats. The goats on the left will receive God's holy wrath due them for their treatment of His chosen people Israel. The sheep on the right, the place of honor in the presence of God, will receive the ultimate favored-nation status and are spared eternal devastation.

God will come through. Though present-day nations seem to pick on Israel endlessly and get away with it, that won't last forever. God will honor the unconditional promises of the Abrahamic covenant and finally curse those who curse the patriarch's line. He's keeping score even now. When God's promise comes full circle and collides with eternal judgment, the Holocaust, the Spanish Inquisition, and the Crusades will appear minor in scope. We are talking about large segments of the Gentile world being lost at one time. Apparently with Israel's endless supply of enemies down through history, the goats far outnumber the sheep. I would imagine that the sheep count is a remnant, while the goat count is enormous.

Words will be replayed:

- Hitler calling the Jews "filthy vermin."
- Bin Laden calling the Jews "monkeys."
- The Grand Mufti of Jerusalem in 1948: "We must make the Jews live in hell."
- Anti-Semitic slogans: "Kill the dirty Jews!"

- The label *shaheed* or "martyrs" for Palestinian murderers of Jews. Saddam Hussein gave cash rewards to the terrorists' families.

The fight for Jerusalem, the city God chose to reside in, will be remembered. Yasser Arafat delivered these words in a South African mosque on May 10, 1994: "The jihad will continue. . . . You have to understand our main battle is Jerusalem. . . . You have to come and fight a jihad to liberate Jerusalem, your precious shrine. . . . No, it is not their capital. It is our capital." Premier Aleksei Kosygin of the Soviet Union in 1967 called Israel "fascists" filled with "atrocities and violence" after they reclaimed their holy city on the final day of the Six-Day War.

The present-day intifada will be seen for what it is as suicide bombers will pay dearly for their demonic zeal to kill Jews on city buses and in crowded marketplaces. Men and women who wired themselves with dynamite measured in pounds will be exposed as cold-blooded killers of God's people. On a recent visit to Israel, we visited a rehabilitation center in Tel Aviv. Seeing soldiers and civilians who will spend their remaining days in hospital beds was an emotional experience for our mission team. A blinded twenty-year-old engaged soldier, a man without his legs, a woman with a horribly burned face. The gruesome side of the endless news stories about another bus explosion brought to light the sad reality of this new holy war. The numbers fly by us almost nightly: ten dead, thirty-four wounded; fourteen dead, twenty-eight wounded. But these are real people, with lives that will never recover from the newest way to get rid of more Jews.

In April of 2002, while preparing to worship at the Garden Tomb in Jerusalem, my prayer partner, Allen Reedall, and I heard a deafening explosion that sounded like it was only across the street. We were wrong. Nearly a mile away, all were deeply saddened to hear that a young Palestinian woman had detonated twenty pounds of dynamite strapped around her waist and neatly hidden under her baggy burqa. Her killing spot was carefully chosen. The crowded Jewish marketplace on Mahane Yehuda Street where Jews were busy buying last-minute items before sundown officially began another Sabbath. Ironically, Colin Powell was a few blocks away from the blast on another diplomatic quest for the elusive peace that once again was evaporating in Israel. Unfortunately, this misguided Muslim woman believed she would be met at heaven's gate by Allah and his prophet Muhammad to receive a reward for her "courageous act." She, too, will have an appointment with the King of Kings in the Kidron Valley and receive her just reward—eternal punishment.

To say "turnabout is fair play" during God's judgment time one day in Jerusalem is to put it mildly.

At Last . . . Deliverance!

In the early years of Israel's spiritual formation, God swiftly and completely judged the nations who cursed His people. During their establishment in the land, people groups that mocked God soon were recorded on God's endangered species list and then died out. After Israel experienced a spiritual defection and went the way of the pagans into wholehearted idolatry, God sent a nation to take them out of their beloved homeland into captivity. The sentence was carried out by the wicked Babylonians, and their prison was located in the ancient home-land of Abraham. Ironically, the place where the promise was given to a future people was the place where God disciplined them seriously. A major shift had occurred, and one must won-der if Israel, while sitting on the banks of the Euphrates River, fully grasped the turnaround. It was so simple:

- God used Israel to punish the nations who had
  rejected Him and His people.

- God now was using the nations to punish Israel, who had rejected Him while being His people.

As far as history goes, the extermination of nations ceased. The Israelites, through their rank disobedience, was no different from the people living all around them. But God kept score. He always does. The Babylonians punished Israel, and then God punished them by collapsing their kingdom. The Medes and the Persians overran the people from the area of present-day Iraq. The capital city fell, and the influence of all these groups became a feeble whimper from the past.

The law of diminishing influence began to take effect. And so presently, nations are not "smote" by God anymore. That's not to say that He couldn't or won't again. But compared to all the smiting that God did in Israel's early days, times have changed. His weapon of choice today appears to be one that slowly removes a nation from prominence to mediocrity over time. While cursing Israel today, a nation may encounter a type of slow leak that reduces the people group in scope and world stature. Muslim nations are marginalized economically; the former Soviet Union collapsed after a century filled with anti-Semitism as a core value.

Even Great Britain, which once boasted "the sun never sets on the British Empire" when describing its world influence, has ceased to be the power it was only decades ago. The sun does set on the British Empire now. Could this be yet another case of how one nation turned its back on Israel and paid dearly for it? Great Britain ended up fighting against the very state it hoped to help create one day. From 1917 to 1948, the English ruled then Palestine and severely restricted the flow of Jewish immigrants to Israel through its famous series of white papers. The six documents spelled certain death for Europe's Jews because they were blocked from a mass immigration and allowed only to trickle back to Israel in small groups. Thousands could have avoided the gas ovens that were already warming up for them throughout the growing Nazi regime. Heavy stuff to say the least, but a promise is a promise, especially when God makes the promise. "[He comes] to sift the nations in a sieve of destruction" (Isa. 30:28b).

OK, enough cursing, smiting, annihilation, and removing of world powers! Has anyone experienced blessing because of blessing God's people Israel? I'm glad you asked! Turn to chapter 3.

Chapter 3

A Promise That Shaped America

*God's road map for a nation's security is found in the
first book of the Bible. It's no coincidence that America soared
to its prominent world position after its all-out support
of Israel becoming a nation again in 1948.*

Road Map to Prosperity

Vacations for the Doyle family have always been a mixed bless-ing. On one hand, it's wonderful getting away from it all, but with six children and two adults in one car, I often feel I need some kind of counseling afterward. Driving for a day with teenage hormones and brother/sister rivalries while crammed in an overstuffed minivan is major combat duty. Our number-one goal, of course, is to get wherever we're going by setting a new land speed record. The quicker we get there, the less chance there is of an all-out mutiny.

One vacation a few years ago, though, was admittedly over the top. We tried to make it from Colorado to Florida in two days. Two days! That's about fourteen hours of driving two days in a row. On our way back to Colorado, my wife, JoAnn, was driving. Let me first say this: JoAnn is my beautiful little Italian bride. She has many wonderful qualities and numerous spiritual gifts. She does, however, struggle with a directional disorder caused by an inability to decipher north from south and east from west.

While cruising through West Texas toward New Mexico, I decided to get a little shut-eye. I was exhausted from two 3:00 A.M. starts, and I told my sweet wife I probably wouldn't fall asleep but only rest. *Wrong!* Before I faded out, I told JoAnn what to do after we hit the big cities of Dumas and Dalhart. "Just go west on 87 into New Mexico, honey."

After sleeping for nearly three hours, I awoke and immediately had a funny feeling as I looked at our surroundings. They didn't look familiar. As I saw the next mileage sign, we were nearly in Boise City, which meant we were really making good time. The only problem was that we weren't going to Boise City. Boise City is in Oklahoma. Boy, were we lost! After the whole car broke into prolonged laughter, we grabbed the map and found our way back toward the Rocky Mountains and headed out of Sooner land. Getting lost can leave you feeling mentally exhausted.

So it was in Old Testament days. In the first book of the Bible, God purposefully laid out a clear road map, which when followed would lead any nation along a path that resulted in abundance, blessing, and prosperity. Throughout the centuries, nations that followed the map and stayed on course experienced everything that God said they would.

A modern-day example of God's all-out blessing is the United States of America. The course of our country was dramatically altered in the last century when American leadership decided to take the plunge and support the reforming nation of Israel. It was risky and decisive for the U.S., but with strong leaders and a national Judeo-Christian thrust at the time, we followed God's map, stayed on the path, and have never looked back. I believe it is the main reason for our rise to the top spot on the world powers list. In about sixty years, America has soared to a prominence never experienced by another nation in history. In short, we are number one in influence, power, and prosperity. The road map took us as a nation exactly where it promised—to the place of blessing. America has faithfully been a blessing to Israel over six decades now, and in turn, God has generously poured out His blessings on us. Following God's road map has not been without conflict, however.

There has always been a fight over which road map we would follow. Significant groups of people have wanted to throw away God's road map, claiming it's outdated and that the benefits are few, if any. Failing to see the power of God's unconditional Abrahamic covenant, they attribute American prominence to intellect alone. We are just smarter than all of the other nations. How sad. This argument is easily shot down when we compare ourselves to the Asian nations that routinely outscore us in academic testing. Why is China not experiencing more prosperity than we are? Admittedly, things are changing in China with its ability to field an extremely cheap labor force. Yet with its failure to bless Israel, China is light years behind us in world influence, economic prosperity, and basic living conditions. We are not smarter than everyone else, but our blessing of Israel overcomes even intellectual shortcomings. God blesses us as a nation because we support Israel, not because of our national IQ.

Anti-Semitism in America

Unfortunately, the other suggested road maps often reeked of anti-Semitism. Their paths called for us to distance ourselves from Israel or to reject her altogether. The battle was birthed during the chaotic first half of the twentieth century. During that time, two world wars were fought, and intertwined in each conflict was the sticky problem of European Jews and their growing desire to reinhabit the biblical land of Israel.

America was in the midst of an upsurge in immigration due to European instability. Irish, Italians, Germans, Poles, and Jews were streaming into Ellis Island in search of the American dream and to escape the economic uncertainty of their native lands. The United States offered jobs—plenty of them. The modern industrialization of the nation was built on the back of a seemingly never-ending labor force that arrived by the shiploads. Instead of New York City becoming a melting pot, in time it became "little Europe" with the various ethnic groups living together. Other American cities experienced similar growth patterns with little homogenization of cultures. Rather than cultures blending together, the majority of people groups occupied a certain turf within their respective cities. As a result of this, many of the old prejudices from Europe traveled with the immigrants and became as strong as they were in the old country. During the 1800s, Jewish immigrants had experienced little or no discrimination. National issues were not particularly applicable to Jews at the time. With the Civil War dominating the century, Jewish immigrants were ignored and for the most part irrelevant. By the 1880s, a wave of German Jews immigrated to America, and when the turn of the century arrived, the seeds of anti-Semitism had already been planted. Things were changing rapidly for the American Jew.

By the 1920s, Jews were the fastest growing ethnic group in the United States. Henry James reflected the mood of the times with his book *The American Scene*, published in 1907, as Jewish families were filling up New York City's lower east side. "Jewry that had burst all bounds . . . the children swarmed above all—here was multiplication with a vengeance . . . . There is no swarming like that of Israel, when once Israel has got a start."[1] Jews were streaming in, and to many New York resembled a twentieth-century promised land. Not many were applauding their arrivals, however. Oscar Handlin wrote, "A great number of Americans became obsessed with the fear of Jews."[2] Within years, Jews were not looked on with favor as hard-working, blue-collar types. They were seen as a threat to America and suspicious, at best. The garment industry had been home to a large Jewish labor force, and many Americans desired for them to remain there with little chance to move up on the social ladder or to explore other employment avenues. This is one of the reasons why so many Jews started their own businesses and eventually became entrepreneurs. What happened to change how American Jews were perceived in the land of the free?

The Power of Print

Anti-Semitism in modern days has deep roots into the soil of Europe and in the nation of Germany in particular. Germany launched repeated attacks on the Hebrew race in the second decade of the twentieth century. The feelings of European resentment toward the Jews began to grow significantly in Germany. In America, the heat was turned up to a boil following widespread distribution of three publications. *The Protocols of the Elders of Zion* was authored in Russia and translated into English in 1920. The translation proved to be a spurious one, but that was revealed after its widespread distribution, and the damage had been done. The book falsely accused Jews of just about everything under the sun.

Another book followed in the same vein. *The Cause of World Unrest* claimed that the Bolshevik Revolution was Jewish in nature, and the real reason behind it was a massive underground effort to destroy Christendom worldwide. Europe's problems were all being hung around Jewish necks, and the masses were duped into believing laughable assumptions: Jews were dangerous, and hostile takeovers were probable wherever they lived.

Interestingly enough, during the current Israeli-Palestinian conflict, the video version of *The Protocols of the Elders of Zion* has been continuously shown in Muslim-dominated countries such as Egypt. The movie, which has several episodes, was shown over three-week periods. It was accepted hook, line, and sinker with no verifiable evidence to support any of the film's outrageous claims by Arabs all over the Middle East region. The propaganda has proven quite effective by making the Jewish race a scapegoat again for everything that has gone wrong in Arab culture itself.

Did Ford Have a Better Idea?

With Americans becoming obsessed with Judaiphobia, the country's most important piece of anti-Semitic literature was yet to come. This book would be authored by an American icon named Henry Ford. The third publication, *The International Jew*, was written by the automobile-manufacturing guru and legendary businessman during the tide of rising anti-Semitism in the 1920s. With a well-known figure like Ford selling a book that capitalized on anti-Jewish fears, the work sold in the millions in a few short years. Again, the book was based on bogus claims that Jews had a calculated plan to take over the world through finance. America's true enemy was the influential Jewish culture that was growing by leaps and bounds and soon to dominate the United States. Jewish immigration had grown to 2.5 million between 1880 and 1925, and it seemed to sound a national alarm across America.

Even Mark Twain, who was normally sympathetic to the plight of the people without a land, got into the act. He quipped this concerning Jews in America: "When I read in the *Encyclopedia Britannica* that the Jewish population of the United States was 250,000, I wrote the editor and explained to him that I was personally acquainted with more Jews than that in my country, and that his figures were without a doubt a misprint for 25 million."[3]

The International Jew swayed a significant portion of Americans to believe that Jews were multiplying out of control and soon all would be lost to this race that bore the guilt of single-handedly wrecking the continent of Europe. Henry Ford was finally forced to stop printing the book in 1927. Today, you can see a copy of it in Jerusalem's Yad Vashem Holocaust Museum in the section titled "Pre-Nazi Anti-Semitism." Again, the damage had been done as Ford was one of the chief architects of American anti-Semitism.

Ford was not deterred one bit by the book ban. Next, he began a newspaper called *The Dearborn Independent*. This slant on American news routinely ripped American Jews every chance it could. All Ford automobile dealerships nationally were ordered to carry the newspaper. Recently while at lunch, I heard a commercial about Ford Motors and how Henry Ford was the first American businessman to pay his workers five dollars a day. In those days, that was a huge step forward in American plants and hailed as a major breakthrough for our labor force. Ford was well loved for this and a leader among leaders. That's why his relentless hatred of Jews proved to be so damaging since it was launched by an American hero. H. L. Mencken, writing for the Michigan-based paper, summarized the publication's intentions with these words, "The case against the Jews is long and damning. . . . It would justify 10,000 times as many pogroms as now go on in the world."[4] A pogrom, of course, is a systematic murdering of a culture. The first one Israel endured was at the hands of an Egyptian pharaoh during the days of Moses. It seems unbelievable that words like Mencken's would emanate from the United States instead of Russia, Germany, or the Muslim-dominated Middle East.

This was serious. Americans were being hit hard with anti-Semitism. What the Jews had encountered throughout history was exactly what they deserved according to their racist accusers. They had it coming, and more was on the way. All of this was being spread throughout the United States, the nation born out of a quest for religious freedom. Jews were now going it alone in many ways. Wall Street and Ivy League schools began to deny Jews jobs that formerly were open to them. There was growing migration to the West Coast, where they were less suspicious to the older institutions that existed on the East Coast. Jewish Americans displayed natural talent in business. They eventually became the primary movers and shakers in the growing movie industry developing in southern California.

America Follows Suit

With all the propaganda creating national panic, something had to be done. Legislation began to emerge in an effort to put a very short leash on American Jews. The Johnson Act of 1924 restricted immigration and began to establish quotas on the less-desired races. At the top of the restriction list were, of course, Jews. Intellectuals who were racially motivated were led by Henry Cabot Lodge of Massachusetts along with Madison Grant and Prescott F. Hall from the South. Their beliefs were that the northern and western Europeans were superior to Mediterraneans, Slavs, Orientals, and especially Jews. English, Irish, German, and Scandinavian people were not restricted in the immigration process; only the undesirables were held back.

The anti-Semitic trend jumped tracks quickly into the business world. Large insurance companies, banks, retail chains, and law firms generally did not hire Jews. By the 1930s, American Jews wanted to venture out of the garment industry into new lines of work, but they were virtually shut out from every possibility. Like a brush fire, discrimination against Jews was spreading everywhere. College teaching jobs and university faculty positions were almost always off limits to Jews. Private colleges and universities began to establish quotas to limit Jewish admissions. Institutions of higher learning fell into the grip of racism. It was most difficult for Jewish students to be accepted at medical schools. This forced many Jews to study abroad. Harvard, the cornerstone of the Ivy League and founded on Christian principles, pushed to implement Jewish limits through a quota system. The plan was voted down by the faculty, but then President Lawrence Lowell allowed it anyway, thereby bypassing the vote.[5]

Charles "Lucky" Lindbergh, the legendary American aviator who successfully flew the first flight over the Atlantic Ocean, hated the Jews. He actually liked Adolf Hitler and portrayed him as a nonthreatening leader after meeting with him in Berlin before World War II. He joined the chorus and claimed that Jews were the most dangerous group in America. He boldly predicted that any U.S. involvement in war would be directly linked to a Jewish push toward it. At an America First rally, he attacked American Jewry, and the ranks were swelling. By 1944, 24 percent of polled Americans regarded Jewish people as "a menace."

In an ironic twist, 85 to 90 percent of Jewish voters backed Franklin D. Roosevelt and openly embraced the New Deal. Some claimed that behind the scenes the New Deal was really the "Jew Deal," but Roosevelt quickly dispelled those rumors with an overt attempt to distance his administration from Jewish Democrats.

In 1939, a low point occurred in the FDR presidency with America's treatment of Jews. Joshua Brandt explained: "The story of the *St. Louis* is an ignominious and often overlooked chapter in the history of the Holocaust and World War II. The ship departed from Hamburg, Germany, in the spring of 1939 and set sail for Cuba. After various anti-Jewish rallies prevented the refugees from settling in Cuba, the ship sailed for the United States. There, too, the ship was turned despite the State Department's awareness of the severity of the situation. The ship later disembarked in four European ports after a month at sea. More than 300 of the passengers eventually perished in the Holocaust."[6]

Over time, America has had to come to grips with what the government allowed to happen to the Jews on that ship. Many of them ended up going to Auschwitz concentration camp. Michael Barak of the United States lost his father as a result of the American president's refusal to do anything about the *St. Louis*. He immigrated to Israel years ago and holds the United States responsible for the death of his father. What perhaps is more shocking to learn from America's failure during World War II is that FDR's administration knew what was going on in Nazi Germany to the defenseless Jews and did nothing. Poland sent a secret envoy to inform the president about the mounting Jewish carnage and still nothing changed. Even U.S. Supreme Court Justice Felix Frankfurter, who was Jewish, heard the same evidence about the Holocaust and remained silent. Perhaps the American leadership did not believe the reports, which must have seemed outrageous. To have heard of thousands of Jews being gassed in several European camps and remaining neutral seems unfathomable. During the Jewish onslaught, an old front began to emerge again in open Jewish attacks. It was the church that stood in line next, awaiting its turn to bash the descendants of Abraham.

Anti-Semitism in the Church

Irish Catholics, who previously had been recipients of widespread discrimination themselves, next joined the chorus of boos leveled at Jewish immigrants. Father Charles E. Coughlin, a very influential Roman Catholic priest, led the way. This new Irish Catholic version of anti-Semitism became the Christian front for the United States. The Jews were getting it from all major sectors of society. Father Coughlin's weekly radio program, which broadcasted into millions of homes across the country, contained Jewish slander and vicious attacks. For Jews wanting to enjoy religious freedom without persecution that had been so prevalent in Russia and Europe, this seemed like the same song, second verse. This was a new kind of assault for American Jews. Unfortunately, it was an old one worldwide for Judaism itself. Sadly, centuries earlier the church had positioned itself as a bitter enemy of the Jewish race.

Off to a Bad Start

In the first century, Jesus' church was in its spiritual formation stage, and several key questions were decided over the next few hundred years. Doctrines of highest importance were debated for decades and then finally formulated. Some of the earliest questions turned into enormous battlegrounds that the church had to maneuver its way through and then define. Questions like:

- Is it proper to fight in a war?
- Was Jesus truly God while at the same time truly man?
- Is Scripture to be read literally or figuratively?
- Was Mary the mother of God?
- Is the Holy Spirit God?

At the same time, the church had questions about Jewish people in general. Even though their Messiah was Jewish and so were the apostles, what was the church to do with Jews? Unfortunately, the church fell into a theological trap door that set the stage for its checkered history. That trap door is unmarked, and many Christians fall for it today. Its name is "replacement theology." In this belief, the church replaces Israel, and the Abrahamic covenantal promises become void due to Israel's disobedience and outright rejection of the Messiah.

Promises, Promises

Even though the church was birthed within Judaism, many Israelites rejected Jesus as Messiah altogether. Israel was confronted with the messianic claims of Jesus of Galilee centuries before, and the Jews passed Him off as a deranged rabbi gone astray. The rejection was thorough as they branded Him a "blasphemer," tortured Him, and murdered Him. God visited His people that He chose out of all the nations to offer them forgiveness of sins, and they led the way in putting Him to death. No plunge into iniquity has ever been any deeper. Obviously, this was an enormous sin that set the stage for the next several centuries of the Jews' tragic history. In Luke 19:44b Jesus Himself predicted a coming Jerusalem catastrophe because of Jewish rejection of Him: "And they will not leave one stone on another in you, because you did not recognize the time of your visitation." The lowest point in Jewish history is not the Holocaust, although six million Jews dying needlessly is certainly nothing to make light of.

The question is whether or not this cancels out the promises of Genesis 12. If the covenant was based on Israel's ability to obey, then replacement theology would be our only option. But even with the most casual reading of the verses, it is clear to see that the burden of fulfillment is on God and not His people. In Genesis 12, God promised it. In Genesis 15, after the animals and birds were cut in half, it was God whose holy presence walked between them to confirm the covenant and personally guarantee it. Abraham had no responsibilities in the covenant. He did not participate in it since he was sleeping and viewed it through a vision. Every part of it was based on Yahweh and rested squarely on His shoulders. The covenant had no conditions. No ifs, no buts.

In other instances, our holy God promised blessing *if* the recipient remained in good stead with Him. The classic biblical example of a conditional covenant like this is the one made to Israel's third royal monarch, King Solomon. The time frame for the promise was during an all-time high point for Israel. Solomon was God's man carefully selected to build the first permanent structure that God would reside in. The previous place God had dwelt in was a portable tent called the tabernacle that was moved several times during Israel's years of wandering in the desert. Those days were over now, and God desired His house to be the heartbeat of His people's existence. King Solomon was given the sacred honor of constructing Israel's first temple. The breathtaking centerpiece of the Holy City would be much more than a place of worship. The temple would define Israel's very existence. Upon completion of this massive task, God appeared to Solomon for the second time in his life:

> The LORD said to him: I have heard your prayer
> and petition you have made before Me. I have conse-
> crated this temple you have built, to put My name
> there forever; My eyes and My heart will be there at
> all times. As for you, if you walk before Me as your
> father David walked, with integrity of heart and
> uprightness, doing everything I have commanded
> you, and if you keep My statutes and ordinances, I
> will establish your royal throne over Israel forever, as
> I promised your father David: You will never fail to
> have a man on the throne of Israel. If you or your
> sons turn away from following Me and do not keep
> My commands—My statutes that I have set before
> you—and if you go and serve other gods and worship
> them, I will cut off Israel from the land I gave them,
> and I will reject the temple I have sanctified for My
> name. Israel will become an object of scorn and
> ridicule among all the peoples. Though this temple is
> [now] exalted, every passerby will be appalled and
> will hiss. They will say: Why did the LORD do this to

this land and this temple? Then they will say:
Because they abandoned the LORD their God who
brought their ancestors out of the land of Egypt.
They clung to other gods and worshiped and served
them. Because of this, the LORD brought all this ruin
on them. (1 Kings 9:3–9)

Clearly, two major ifs were embedded in the promise. If Solomon walked with God, his lineage would have a continuous ruler on Israel's throne, but if he or his sons turned from God, then Israel's days in the Promised Land would be numbered. Solomon did turn from God. In a selfish attempt to gain power no matter the cost, he married foreign wives in an effort to expand his burgeoning kingdom. In the Middle East, an ancient expression found its way into Solomon's thinking; "trade follows the bride" worked well in the king's life. The more he married foreign princesses, the more his kingdom grew. Solomon forged alliances with all the important kings around him by simply marrying their daughters. This "all in the family" approach to doing business lavished wealth and prestige on the nation of Israel. The glory days were here, and Solomon's strategic economic formula made him the fair-haired king of the known world. Israel enjoyed being the lead nation of the world, but it wouldn't last long, and its prosperity came with a price it was unprepared to pay. The Israelites were rejected by God, and their kingdom eventually disintegrated as they were carried away into two forced captivities. Solomon succeeded in opening up trade routes virtually everywhere through his multiple marriages. But the trade routes that traveled to pagan nations were also conduits to export idolatry back into Israel. Satan carefully crafted a spirit of "religious tolerance" in Israel, and God's holy nation finally crumbled.

God guaranteed that if Solomon went too far, everything promised was off. He did, and Israel's crash proved to be complete as Jerusalem was sacked and the people were carted off to live in the pagan capital of Babylon. That's a conditional covenant.

God's promise to Abraham, however, had no strings, escape clauses, or conditions. Since it was based on God's unchanging nature called immutability, it could not be reversed.

The Early Church's Anti-Semitism

Somehow the unconditional covenant with Abraham was rationalized and quickly forgotten by the early church. Church fathers who helped forge direction and shape doctrine led their followers into anti-Semitism. Some of their thoughts on Jews are chilling to say the least:

- Justin: "Kill the Jews."
- Chrysostom: "Kill the pigs."
- Origen: "The synagogue is a brothel."

How sad the heart of God must have been! The church is to be the best friend Israel has. Paul in Romans 10 said that Jesus' church was to be the instrument God used to bring Jews to God. The Jews would envy our living relationship with God and become envious and then turn to Him in repentance. Paul went on to drive the point home in Romans 11:1 with this question for us, the church: "I ask then: Did God reject his people? By no means" (NIV). The words "by no means" are an excellent translation of the Greek word *meganointa*, which answers the question of a possible Jewish rejection with "never"! Apparently, God's emphasis on His plan for the Jewish people fell on deaf ears. Over time, church leaders continued to use heavy artillery in dealing with Jews worldwide. The term "vermin" did not originate with Adolf Hitler but shockingly with the great leader of the Reformation movement—Martin Luther.

So when Father Coughlin in the 1930s began slandering American Jewish immigrants, it was nothing new. He merely was following an unholy church tradition of tearing down God's chosen people. *Encyclopedia Judaica* concurs that Coughlin's words were every bit as convincing and persuasive as Henry Ford's were.

WWII—Dark Days for Jews, Dark Days for the Church

The central figure that set the pace for an outright rejection of the Jews was seated in Rome, and he was unmoved by the desperate cries for help. His name was Eugenio Pacelli, Pope Pius XII. As leader of the Catholic Church from 1939 to 1958, he not only failed to speak out about Hitler's Final Solution; he formed an alliance with the century's most evil figure that ensured the fate of European Jews.

In *Hitler's Pope*, author John Cornwell cataloged the tragic reign of one of the Catholic Church's leaders. In the days before his papal rule, Pacelli was a lawyer who played a major role in Catholic theology and politics. In the 1920s, he served as papal nuncio in Berlin. A nuncio is a high-ranking Vatican official who acts much like a foreign ambassador to a particular country. Eugenio Pacelli was quite familiar with Nazi ideology and eventually came into a strategic relationship with the rising Adolf Hitler. The relationship was a warm one, evidenced by the fact that Germany contributed more money to the Vatican than any other nation. In fact, "Germany had donated more funds to the Holy See than all other nations of the world put together."[7] This startling fact led to an agreement between Germany and the Vatican that would deliver economic prosperity to the Catholic Church. The deal was advantageous for Germany as it clearly spelled out that the Nazis would rise unopposed by the most powerful Catholic community in the world. In 1933, then serving as a cardinal, Eugenio Pacelli negotiated the *Reich Concordat* with Hitler. Cornwell drew his information from

Vatican and Jesuit archives that clearly outline the agreement. Privately, Hitler claimed that when the Catholic Church rolled over in compliance with the Nazis, the dye was cast for Jewish eradication.

By Protestants the case can easily be made that Pope Pius XII did not represent the majority of Christians. Unfortunately, this objection matters very little to Jews who collectively lost one-third of their race in the Holocaust. Not only does it matter little to Jews, but historically it doesn't hold up either. Certainly, it is easy for us to distance ourselves from him, but did evangelicals stand up en masse against the demonically infested empire of the Third Reich? No, again.

These are some of the most painful issues that we as Christians can ever face. We can try to explain it away, but there fails to be a reasonable explanation. Evil flourished in the midst of church apathy toward the horrendous plight of God's chosen people. Years of pain, suffering, and murder passed by unopposed as we, the church, watched it all unfold. It is very easy for us in hindsight to point fingers and lay the blame on others. In my heart I know that I must ask myself, "Would I have done anything?"

While speaking to the Hadassah Jewish Women's Group of Albuquerque in 2002, I decided to face history head-on and asked the largely Jewish audience to forgive us as Christians for one of the worst examples of passivity ever. We will make strides in Jewish outreach only when we show a change of heart throughout the years in dealing with anti-Semitism in the future. It will arise again. On the horizon, a global hatred for Jews will culminate one day on Jerusalem's doorstep with hopes of Jewish annihilation forever. The Lord Jesus will intervene at that time, and anti-Semitism will be eradicated forever. But for now, back to World War II.

In *Hitler's Cross*, pastor Erwin Lutzer took us deep inside the church during the height of Nazi Germany. Seeing himself as some sort of Aryan savior, Hitler substituted the government of Germany for the church. During these days the lines of distinction between the church and the Third Reich blurred until they were invisible. Lutzer reluctantly wrote these condemning words: "Hatred for the Jews, I'm sorry to say, also flourished within the churches."[8] For evangelical believers, it's more pleasant to remember heroes like Dietrich Bonhoeffer, Corrie ten Boom, and Martin Niemöller. Bonhoeffer, a pastor and Nazi resister whose classic book *The Cost of Discipleship* is still inspiring Christians, was executed on Hitler's gallows. Corrie ten Boom, who with her family helped innocent Jews escape via their secret hiding place, spent several years in Ravensbruck concentration camp. Martin Niemöller, another pastor, was sentenced to Dachau concentration camp until he was set free by Allied troops at the end of World War II.

These stories are exceptions, though, as by and large the German church was completely deceived. In Lutzer's book, the chapter "The Church Is Dismembered" delineates how organized opposition to Hitler was all but impossible. Germany had now rebounded from its humiliating World War I defeat. The economy was exceptionally strong. German national pride was at an all-time high. Dr. Werner, Hitler's deputy for church relations, sent a letter to all German pastors in 1938, calling them to swear absolute allegiance to the Führer. Later that year, the *Chicago Tribune* ran an article titled "Bible Twisted to Nazi Creed." The story uncovered Reich Bishop Ludwig Miller's rewrite of the Sermon on the Mount and the entire Gospel of John that was more favorable to the mood of the day. "The words *sin* and *grace* were deleted from the texts, and the Golden Rule was rewritten to apply only to relationships between Nazi comrades. All references to Old Testament prophets, from Moses to Abraham were also deleted. Everlasting life was defined as 'true life.'"[9]

The pressure on the church was enormous, and the German body of Christ imploded. Crosses were now being replaced by swastikas on most churches. During Holy Week, 1938, one bishop sent an enthusiastic telegram to Hitler with news that a great historic time had arrived. All the pastors in his district had obeyed a command and "have with joyful hearts taken an oath of loyalty to Fuhrer and Reich. . . . One God, One obedience to the faith. Hail my Fuhrer!"[10] With church and state now walking hand in hand, anti-Semitism was the official stance of Germans whether they were Christians or not. During the "Night of Broken Glass" (*Kristallnacht*), when 177 synagogues were destroyed and twenty thousand Jews arrested, the church fell silent. No outrage was expressed.

Muted into oblivion, the church of Germany was marginalized during its greatest hour of need. Jews would be seized and taken off to die by the millions, and the church sadly sat by and watched. In one church during worship each Sunday, parishioners clearly heard screams from trains filled with Jews headed for death camps. Week after week the hideous sound interrupted the church service. Finally, the pastor had the people sing loudly during the exact time the train would pass the church, drowning out the cries of Jewish victims on the way to the slaughter. How sad! How indicting! Would we have joined the few resisters, or would we have just sung louder to avoid dealing with it all? The head of the Gestapo described the church this way: "The situation in the churches is characterized by weariness with struggle, by uncertainty of purpose, and by lack of courage."[11] Lutzer's closing words pierce the heart of every follower of Jesus Christ: "If only the church had seen that when the Jews were persecuted, it was the Lord Jesus who was suffering."[12] Even more so, those who stood against the Nazis and faced imprisonment or death are to be remembered with honor. Their awards await them in heaven.

D-Day—The Real One

Now that you know how widespread anti-Semitism was during the first half of the twentieth century and how Germans, Americans, Catholics, and Protestants got caught up in it, the conviction that U.S. President Harry Truman had to help Jews establish Israel as their homeland is all the more remarkable. Certainly there was sentiment after the Jewish devastation of World War II to help them find a home and end their wandering after nineteen centuries. Yet, with so many American lives lost during the conflict, the mood just as easily could have been to blame the Jews for it all.

The American failures were obvious with pictures of living skeletons being liberated from the death camps. The photographs shocked the world as the rumors of what was going on under the Nazi regime paled in comparison to real life. The collective guilt people of conscience felt left many Americans wondering what to do with the decimated house of David. President Roosevelt died in April of 1945, and Jews, who seem to be able to forgive and forgive again, mourned the death of the four-term president. It would be decades before the truth was revealed about the extent of the president's knowledge of the Holocaust while it was in full swing. Would the next American president do anything to change the nation's course? The next president did indeed do that. Harry Truman turned out to be the man who would single-handedly change the direction of America.

President Harry Truman was the first American leader to risk his political livelihood by answering the call to lend a hand in helping Jewish survivors return to their biblical homeland as the reconstituted nation of Israel. As mentioned in chapter 1, the United Nations' proposed resolution for a Jewish homeland was so hotly contested that Truman had to use his influence to garner the last few votes needed to pass the historic vote in 1947.

This was an American president's finest hour. In chapter 1, we looked at the political pressure Truman placed on Greece, Haiti, Liberia, and the Philippines in order to convince them to vote for the new Jewish state in November of 1947. In *O Jerusalem* we learn:

> The United States, again acting on the instigation of the White House, threw the full impact of its tremendous prestige behind the Jewish cause. Two justices of the United States Supreme Court personally cabled Philippine President Carlos Rojas warning that "the Philippines will isolate millions and millions of American friends if they continue in their efforts to vote against partition." Twenty-six senators cabled Rojas and urged him to change his nation's vote. The Philippine ambassador was summoned to a blunt but intensive briefing at the White House. Finally, Rojas ordered his delegation "in the higher national interest" to switch its vote from "against" to "for" partition.[13]

A Thanksgiving recess for the United Nations began the Wednesday before the official vote on November 29, 1947. This allowed more pressure and more communication with the nations that were needed to swing the vote Israel's way. A two-thirds majority was needed to pass the proposal. Twenty-two votes were needed, and President Truman turned up the heat even more with intense political pressure. *O Jerusalem* continues: "By direct order of the White House, the United States had exerted every form of pressure available to it on those nations in the United Nations opposed to partition or hesitant in their support of it. President Truman had personally warned the United States delegate to the United Nations, Herschel Johnson, to 'd—— well deliver the partition vote or there will be hell to pay.' His advisor Bernard Baruch had shocked France's United Nation's delegate Alexandre Parodi with a blunt threat to cut United States aid if France opposed partition."[14] Truman was in rare form! The pressure was working, and Israel was voted a nation again by the United Nations by twenty-three in favor, thirteen against, and ten abstentions. The vote to divide Palestine and give a portion of it back to its ancient inhabitants, Israel, was now a reality.

Chaim Weizmann, who had been the leader of the Zionist movement for decades and had been the one to persuade President Truman to support the Jewish state, was not able to attend. The severity of the moment complete with its historical significance leveled him with emotion. He was not able to leave his hotel room and attend the reading of the votes. He sat alone with his radio, sobbing uncontrollably.

Golda Meir, the future prime minister of Israel, sat in Jerusalem with a notepad in her lap, keeping a tally of the votes. At one point, her tears had so flooded her notepad that she was no longer able to read her own writing.

The reaction of the Syrian delegate to the United Nations was quite the opposite, of course. With chilling accuracy, he boldly proclaimed that the holy places of Jerusalem would now become a place of war. He also rightly predicted that peace would be absent from the area for generations.

Put Your Money Where Your Mouth Is

During the 1940s, it is clear that God was moving powerfully throughout the earth. The war was over, and now that the Nazi war machine was destroyed, the question of a Jewish homeland had to be addressed. Several waves of *aliyah* (immigration) had already brought thousands of Jews back to what was then called Palestine. Alternatives were suggested as a homeland for the Jews in an effort to avoid confronting the ultimate political nightmare. At one point, Uganda had been offered by Great Britain as a possible new promised land for the Zionists. But Israel was the only place ever considered by the Jewish leadership. Israel was the land of the Hebrew nation. Jewish roots were deeply buried in the soil of Israel 3,400 years before, and try as they might, the nations of the world could not extract them. A Jew belonged in Israel. For centuries, the phrase "next year in Jerusalem" filled Jewish hearts with hope to keep their belief alive that one day they would return home.

President Harry Truman halted the tidal wave of anti-Semitism in America and, in so doing, changed the course of the United States. By blessing Israel, America's course was set for its meteoric rise to prominence among the nations of the world. The post-World War II leader impacted America more than he could ever have known. On May 14, 1948, Israel became a nation again—brought back from the dead. Our American president was the first world leader to officially recognize Israel as a state. On the next page is a copy of the actual note from President Truman about the historical event.

The course of history was radically changed for Jews and Americans alike. Obviously, this was very unpopular with Arabs worldwide. America had oil interests in the Middle East, and its partnership with the Arabian American Oil Company (ARAMCO) was threatened with the rebirth of the Jewish nation. Amazingly, one of history's bastions of anti-Semitism, the Soviet Union, actually voted for the Jewish state. In retrospect, the Soviets probably thought that Israel would either be Socialist or even Communist since kibbutz life is based on principles of shared community. Not long after the founding of the state of Israel, the Soviets dumped their support and sided with the oil-rich Arab nations of the region. The hand of God was evident in bringing Jewish people in throngs back to their beloved Israel. On May 14, 1948, the rebirth of the nation of Israel officially began. It was 4:00 P.M. in Tel Aviv, and David Ben-Gurion, soon to be Israel's first prime minister, read these words that

This Government has been informed that a Jewish state has been proclaimed in Palestine, and recognition has been requested by the *provisional* Government thereof.

The United States recognizes the provisional government as the de facto authority of the new *State of Israel.*

Harry Truman

Approved.
May 14, 1948.

6.11

http://www.trumanlibrary.org/photos

reverberated around the world: "In the Land of Israel, the Jewish people came into being. In this land was shaped their spiritual, religious, and national character. Here they lived in sovereign independence. Here they created a culture of national and universal import and gave to the world the eternal Book of Books." The bones of Ezekiel 37 were no longer dead and dry; Jewish life was being breathed into the ancient land of Israel again.

America has for the most part been true to Israel ever since its rebirth in 1948. While the United Nations has frequently opposed the tiniest Middle East nation in a majority of its rulings, the United States has supported Israel. Over the years, America has helped Israel develop technology to defend itself. Like a big brother, the United States has at times been Israel's sole backer. Billions of dollars are sent from the U.S. treasury to Israel each year to help the Israelis finance the enormous cost of being the area's only democracy, while existing and thriving in the midst of so many hostile nations. However, Islamic-dominated nations are not the only ones ganging up on Israel. Routinely, these powerful groups also speak out against Israel: the Vatican, the World Council of Churches, the United Nations, the European Union, the Arab League, China, Russia, and American Islamic groups.

During the decades of faithful blessing of Israel, the United States has become the world's superpower. God's gifts have given America status that it never could have enjoyed had it failed to support Israel. The billions we have invested in God's chosen people have been much like a tithe to God. The more we have invested in Israel, the more God has blessed us. In Malachi 3:10b, God says, "See if I will not open the floodgates of heaven and pour out a blessing for you without measure." This premier passage on tithing sounds very much like the results of our continual blessing of God's people of Israel. The promise found way back in the first book of the Bible to Abraham is the foundation by which our American nation has been shaped. Israel and America over the past fifty years truly have become two nations under God.

★ ✡ ★ ✡

Hanna—The Shepherd

BEING A PASTOR IS TOUGH and demanding. Being a pastor in the West Bank of Israel is all of that and dangerous as well. Since Christians are for the most part considered friends of Israel, Islamic leadership continually threatens believers. In Bethlehem, Palestinian Christians are often badgered about becoming Muslims. Bethlehem Bible College students are known in the town where Jesus was born, and Muslims are relentless in their recruitment of them. "Why don't you give up? Come over to our side. In the end, we're going to win." In Gaza, believers are under constant scrutiny and choose their words carefully on the street. One brother recently had his apartment ransacked by Islamic spies. A friend of his said there was such a commotion in the place that other neighbors peeked in the window. They spotted an Islamic cleric watching the television as his assistants tore the place apart!

Such is the life of the Bible-believing, Jesus-loving Palestinians in Israel. They are caught between the proverbial rock and hard place.

In Arab culture, there is a strong Christian tradition that predates the birth of Islam by seven centuries. The Coptic Church, for example, has a long history and is accepted in Egypt despite Islam's overall control of the nation. Christian, as I've said before, doesn't necessarily mean born-again believer. It's often used only as a designation for a non-Muslim born in an Arab family. All of this is accepted within the Arab world. Formerly part of Iraq's government, Tariq Aziz is a Christian. Yasser Arafat's wife, Suhad, is too. Does this mean they are born-again believers? Probably not. What separates nominal Christians from believers in the Middle East are two fundamental distinctions:

Believers:

1.   Have a born-again experience with Jesus.

2.   Have a desire to convert anyone who has not had a born-again conversion. This includes Muslims as well.

Herein is the rub. Believers are evangelistic. Nominal Christians are not. Nominal Christians can coexist with Muslims easily here. Believers cannot. They actively form relationships with Muslims in an effort to rescue them from the darkness of their sin. Believers inevitably clash with Muslims in the Middle East over this.

Hanna shepherds the flock under his care right in the heart of this spiritual showdown. He is a pastor's pastor. He has a gentle spirit that is memorable. He grew up in the area and decided he would pursue his education in the United States. God had tugged at his heart, and he was determined to not be one of the many who left the West Bank to study abroad never to return. Before he departed for a California seminary, he promised his father he would return. God taught Hanna two important lessons, which he learned outside the classroom. They would mark him and prepare him to lead the sheep through the hostile spiritual terrain they call home. The two lessons were:

1.   Hanna's father died right after he enrolled in seminary. Would he go back, get absorbed in his life, and never return? He had responsibilities now being the only son. Hanna made sure his mother and sisters were safe, provided for, and cared for. God had called him to serve as a shepherd, and he could not forsake his Master's voice. He buried his father and returned to his training.

2.   Hanna ran out of money. He wasn't able to pay for graduate school up front, and the enormous cost on a modest Palestinian budget was out of the question. He

had been under the impression that he could do a work study program and pay as he went. He asked the Lord what to do. The answer he received surprised him for sure. A Jews for Jesus conference was in town, and Hanna called an area representative and explained to him his predicament. How humbling it was for Hanna. Where he lived, Jews were the no-good enemy of the Palestinian people. All of life's problems were because of "these dirty Jews"!

The Jews for Jesus leader was used by God more than he ever could have comprehended. He told Hanna to come to the meeting that night and invited him to share his story. The messianic leader called the faithful to prayer and then took up an offering for Hanna. "We need to help this Palestinian brother, folks. He is going to be a pastor in the West Bank."

The offering was over $10,000. Hanna was overwhelmed. So were the messianic brothers and sisters who took care of the entire first year of seminary. On that day, Jewish believers paid for a Palestinian brother to follow the call of God and study for ministry.

Hanna now shepherds the flock with great care in the midst of a battle zone. He is diligently preparing a core of young men for the ministry. He is a disciple. He is a leader. His humble, unassuming demeanor is in stark contrast to the mafia-style leadership all around him. He is quietly preparing the next generation of leaders for the believing church. He baptizes new converts to Christ. He does premarriage counseling and performs weddings. He loves his people, and the feeling is mutual. Above all, he is a faithful laborer in the field for Jesus. His life has been threatened by Islamic terror-spreading groups, yet he remains unfazed. He has a charge from God to reach the lost sheep of Judea and Samaria. He is God's man for the West Bank.

★ ☆ ★ ☆

*Therefore, as a fellow elder and witness to the sufferings of
the Messiah, and also a participant in the glory about to
be revealed, I exhort the elders among you: shepherd God's
flock among you, not overseeing out of compulsion but
freely, according to God's [will]; not for the money but eagerly;
not lording it over those entrusted to you, but being examples
to the flock. And when the chief Shepherd appears, you
will receive the unfading crown of glory.*

1 PETER 5:1–4

Section 2

SORTING OUT
THE MIDDLE EAST MAZE

The solution to the Middle East powder keg is
the church of Jesus Christ. Only He can transform the
hearts of Arabs and Jews. No peace treaties or extra
amounts of international pressure will change a thing.
Only Jesus can save His homeland.

Chapter 4

Dangerous Alliances

Currently, nations are realigning, forming new partnerships that will end in a regional Arab-Israeli war. This disaster will destabilize the world and spark a new holy war.

Deep Wounds

As Americans, we have relatively short memories. In our history as a nation, we quickly normalize relations with former enemies only a few years after being at war with them. During the birth of our nation, Great Britain was the feared evil empire of the day. The British invasion originally had nothing to do with the Beatles, the Rolling Stones, or the Dave Clark 5, but with England's famous redcoat army that fought us in one of our nation's bloodiest conflicts. "The British are coming" were the feared words of the day. Today, Great Britain is one of our most trusted allies worldwide. Our war wounds have healed, and relatively little animosity exists between the two nations.

During World War II, Germany and Japan fought against us and claimed thousands of U.S. lives in Europe and in the South Pacific. From Normandy to Pearl Harbor, American soldiers were killed and wounded defending our freedom from tyrannical world leaders who tried in vain to defeat us. My father served in the United States Army Air Corp, flying in B-17s as a radioman while America made its way into Europe through France. The lives lost fighting the Axis powers were not sacrificed in vain. Hitler was stopped, and the Japanese invasion was also, as America successfully defended democracy on two fronts in the turbulent 1940s.

Today, Germany and Japan are both forgiven and important allies for the United States. The regimes that drove them into a global conflict are long gone, and both nations that formerly despised us have firmly adopted our democratic ways. Apart from the recent war with Iraq, Germany has been a strong ally for years, and so has Japan. World War II is long gone. The wounds have healed. Forgiveness exists.

In the Middle East, however, forgiveness is rare and wounds run deeper. Wars that concluded thousands of years ago still carry latent hostilities that are as strong today as ever. While traveling to the Middle East the first time, I quickly found out that a major stumbling block in the Arab Muslim evangelism was a period in Christian history called the Crusades. Fueled by Pope Urban II's desire to establish Jerusalem as a Christian city, various "church armies" made their way to the Middle East beginning in 1095. Their goal was to recover the Holy Land from the Muslims. Three waves of crusaders all coming from Europe extended the wars from 1095 to 1291. This dark chapter of church history was an abysmal failure. Thousands of Muslims, Jews, and Christians died needlessly. The church lowered itself by trading salvation by grace for salvation by force. The Crusades backfired on all fronts. In the end, the church appeared to be no different from Islam in its approach to world evangelization. The last battle was fought in 1291 in the coastal town of Acre. But Christian domination and control of Jerusalem ended when Saladin, the great Islamic general from Turkey, defeated the Christian army near the Sea of Galilee at the Hattin in 1187. Other attempts were made over the next century. The famous Richard the Lionhearted of England fought and regained some ground but not Jerusalem itself. "The Crusades joined together two themes which were developing strongly in eleventh century Europe: the Holy War, or military expedition blessed by the church, and the pilgrimage to a holy place. The journey of a Christian army to recover the Holy Land from the Muslims fulfilled both of these."[1] Shockingly, it is common to meet Muslims in the Middle East who still hold the Crusades against Christians as if they were fought last week rather than eight hundred years ago. The unforgiveness will not seem to go away. Like a bad cup of Turkish coffee, the Crusades left an awful taste in the mouths of millions of Muslims worldwide. So it is in Israel and in the Middle East, where, certainly, bitterness permeates an unsteady history.

Today's political commentators often try to settle the Middle East maze of conflict without allowing any room for the enormous religious and historical roots that run all the way back to the first book of the Bible, or 4,100 years ago. In this area, old scores are settled over and over again. And speaking of old scores, some followers of Islam have plenty of them in their eyes to settle with both Christians and Jews. When it comes to Christians, Saladin still fights the Crusaders. When it comes to Jews, Ishmael still fights Isaac.

Islamic Agenda

The Muslims have had another active battlefront with Jews for thirteen centuries. If it were not for the Abrahamic covenant promised to the descendants of Isaac, Jews would have been wiped out centuries ago. How is it that in the last fifty-six years Jews have not only survived but have thrived while being surrounded by Muslims who outnumber them nearly ten to one? God's miraculous intervention has continuously sustained them. True to form, the descendants of Ishmael have lived in hostility toward their brothers. Despite the incredible odds in their favor, Israel's surrounding nations have failed to achieve solidarity and have not only hated the Jews but have hated each other. With differing interests, a comprehensive plan has yet to emerge from the region's Islamic nations. They lack two things as of yet: a common goal and a unifying leader.

The common goal has started to become clear from Cairo all the way to Baghdad in the last few years. The goal is to take Jerusalem under Islamic control. The phrase "final status" is all about Jerusalem and what will ultimately happen to the city itself. This is the common goal that will unify Muslims not only in the Middle East but worldwide.

To Islam, control is everything. The advancement of the Islamic empire globally has been a textbook example of systematic seize-and-control land acquisitions. No piece of earth yet to be taken is even close in importance to the city of Jerusalem. How can Islam call Jerusalem its third holiest city and fail to have complete control over it? To prove the superiority of the faith of all Muslims, Jerusalem is the ultimate test of the power of Islam.

The deepest wounds Islam has experienced in the last century have been, in truth, self-inflicted. All that Israel has accomplished during its brief existence is galling to followers of Islam. Since the Jews' return, the achievements are quite remarkable. Here is a partial list:

The Desert Has Bloomed

For four hundred years under Islamic Turkish rule, Israel was a treeless wasteland. Gone was the land of milk and honey that God promised to the Jewish slaves of Egypt in Exodus. The land is a good land that God gave to His covenant people Israel. The phrase "the land of milk and honey" speaks of the inherent beauty and its subsequent crops that would burst forth with productivity. With Israel in its dispersion and Muslims ruling the land, swamps emerged and trees were cut down. With Israel back, more than 100 million trees have been planted, the swamps are long gone, and the harvests are again lush and abundant. The malaria-infested area of northern Israel is now beautiful again. "A swampland until the twentieth century, the

Jezreel Valley was drained in the 1920s by Zionist pioneers and now is one of Israel's major agricultural breadbaskets."[2]

The "green line" that marks Israeli territory is green because plants are growing on the Israeli side. In most areas, they are not growing on the Arab side. The reason for all the green within Israel is because Judaism values it. Islam does not. Oh that God would liberate the beautiful Arab culture from Islam's life-squelching choke hold! Israel is only one of three countries worldwide that is self-sufficient and has no need to import anything to feed its growing population. Israel is a slice of paradise in the midst of the Middle East's sweltering sand.

Arabs Have Rights!

Since Israel is a democracy, Arabs who remained in the land and became citizens enjoy life more than in any other country of the region. Israel is the only country in the Middle East where Arabs can vote. Did you catch the full impact of that statement? Arab Israelis who have applied for citizenship vote in all elections. As one commercial says, "Membership has its privileges," and so it goes in Israel. Trading in the "Palestinian" nametag for the "Arab Israeli" one makes a world of difference in any Arab family's lifestyle. They are represented well within the Knesset. They even receive free health care. About one-fifth of Israel is Arab, and these citizens retain the same rights and privileges as its Jewish citizens do. In East Jerusalem, where Arab residents share fears of a coming corrupt Palestinian state, many Arabs have applied for Israeli citizenship. I find this amazing in light of the fact that the Grand Mufti of Jerusalem has threatened death to anyone who makes application. In fact, so many Palestinians applied for Israeli citizenship in the past few years the government has now closed that window of opportunity. Israel feared that within a decade their state would have an Arab majority. Arab citizens of Israel have it made compared to Arab citizens of all other Middle East countries. Arabs who live in Palestinian-controlled areas of Israel have no rights whatsoever. Arab-Israeli Muslims experience the rarest lifestyle found in the Middle East—one of freedom and democracy.

Refugees Are Assimilated

When nations began to form in the Middle East during the 1930s and 1940s, the culture of each and every country changed drastically. The Jews left. Every Arab nation became hostile to its Jewish population. A great refugee problem was birthed. More than 900,000 Jews were forced to leave the countries where they had lived for generations. With Jews returning to Israel, they were no longer welcome in Syria, Iraq, Jordan, and all the other Islamic countries. Israel opened its arms and gladly welcomed all Jewish refugees without hesitation.

Wealth Is for All

Israel has developed a thriving economy even while being preoccupied with defending itself against the surrounding hostile nations. Though the Israelis possess no oil, they have become world leaders in technology, farming, tourism, and education. Israel, for example, is the world leader in diamond production. It is amazing since diamonds are not unearthed in Israel but rather are imported from Africa. The "princess cut" was invented in Israel along with a computerized method of cutting diamonds perfectly. This industry has become the number-one moneymaker in Israel today. Jobs are plentiful as the tiny nation puts to work its endless flow of immigrants who arrive on a daily basis. What a contrast to the oil-wealthy Muslim states that purposefully keep their citizens economically destitute while a privileged few hoard the billions of dollars that flow through their oil pipelines.

Of course, the ultimate goal of Islam is to dominate not only the Middle East but the entire world. Islamic leaders make no attempt to camouflage this. One of the modern jihad promoters of Islam is Mawlana Abul Ala Mawdudi of Pakistan. He is considered a scholar and a leader throughout the Islamic world. He summarized Islam this way: "Islam is not a normal religion like the other religions in the world, and Muslim nations are not like normal nations. Muslim nations are very special because they have a command from Allah to rule the entire world and to be over every nation of the world." He went on to say, "Islam is a revolutionary faith that comes to destroy any government made by man. Islam doesn't look for a nation to be in better condition than another nation. Islam doesn't care about the land or who owns the land. The goal of Islam is to rule the entire world and submit all of mankind to the faith of Islam. Any nation or power in this world that tries to get in the way of that goal, Islam will fight and destroy. In order for Islam to fulfill that goal, Islam can use every power available every way it can be used to bring worldwide revolution. This is jihad."[3] No rules are brought to the table when it comes to Islam and jihad. This is the ultimate end-justifies-the-means religion. The name of the game is conquest.

Fundamentalist Islam projects a takeover of America by the year 2020, according to Islamic expert Dr. Robert Morey. One month after September 11, 2001, in a message titled "Christianity's Response to Islam," Dr. Morey shared this in a La Mesa, California, church. The formula is a simple one—a birthrate that exceeds everyone else's. Muslims traditionally have very large families. In areas like Western Europe that promote small families and have liberalized abortion laws, it is easy to see why Muslim population growth skyrockets while the rest of Europe inches along slowly. In Russia, the numbers are staggering as many Russians have one child while Muslims may have as many as ten.

However, the great success story of the Middle East is Israel not Islam. Muslim states privately seethe at Israel's golden touch. Without their oil, they would be insignificant third-world countries. All of this is not a result of Arab culture but rather is a result of the religion of Islam. Islam enslaves, controls, and seeks to squash any democratic possibilities. The religion has failed to advance its culture since its inception in the eighth century. Muslim nations of the Middle East, though, have enough oil to turn the table and level the playing field no matter how prosperous Israel becomes. In their eyes, they hold the ultimate trump card.

Oil, Oil, Oil

The discovery of oil has produced numerous rags-to-riches stories worldwide. Saudi Arabia is perhaps the most classic picture of this. This country is a huge desert and home to some of the hottest recorded temperatures. It is also home to Islam's two most holy cities—Mecca and Medina. Saudi Arabia is the world's largest oil producer. Its oil influence dominates our globe, and its primary dependents are found in the West. East truly does meet West when it comes to oil deals. Though Saudi Arabia has a small army and has yet to enter a war with Israel, it provides financial backing to the nations that do take on the Zionist enemy. The house of Saud has a wise strategy when it comes to dealing with Israel. The Saudis routinely help arm countries like Syria and Iraq with their vast wealth that pours into other countries' banks day after day.

Saudi Arabia can buy the most sophisticated weapons available anywhere. And it does. Since it is a power broker in the financial world, it appears on the surface to be preoccupied with economic growth and not fighting a holy war. Yet as September 11 taught us, Saudi Arabia was where most of the terrorists were from, and anti-American sentiments are high there. Business is still business, but the Saudis are the major influence in the entire Middle East region whether or not they ever fire one shot at Israel. Dave Dolan wrote, "With petrol dollars inundating Saudi coffers, the government went on a military buying spree in the mid-1970s. Over 63 billion dollars were spent in just the seven years before the preliminary Oslo accord was signed in 1993. The Saudis also doled out a couple billion dollars for Iraqi military purchases before the Gulf War and financed weapons for Syria before and after the conflict. Among other things, Saudi aid has been used in Damascus to purchase North Korean-made Scud missiles. The desert kingdom also helped finance the PLO, especially before Saddam Hussein's invasion of Kuwait."[4] Because of Saudi business sense, the Saudis seem to be friends of the United States. Pictures of sheiks driving their latest Mercedes or BMW give the appearance that the Saudi kingdom is a desert version of Beverly Hills.

The financial strength of the country puts it at the top of the list in the Middle East in terms of worldwide clout and influence. Saudi Arabia is revered and honored by one billion Muslims worldwide as the birthplace of Muhammad and Islam. Mecca and Medina are the "twin cities" of Islam and are woven into the fabric of the religion itself. These holy cities receive millions of observant Muslims every year making their spiritual pilgrimage. Mecca is a forbidden city for any non-Muslim. Christians, Jews, or nonreligious people cannot set foot in Mecca and are considered infidels. To violate this law would guarantee a death sentence. Anti-American feelings are strong in Saudi Arabia for two major reasons:

1. Our support of Israel: Saudis believe that the United States gives Israel everything it wants and that our support signifies a hatred of Arabs and Islam. The fact that we give enormous financial aid yearly in the billions to Egypt, Jordan, and even the Palestinian National Authority is overlooked.

2. Our supposed desecration of Saudi Arabia: During the Gulf War, American soldiers were on Saudi soil. To be sure, Mecca and Medina were not "defiled," yet the sight of America launching a war with an Arab Islamic nation was more than religious Muslims could stomach. Osama bin Laden used this as the very reason for his vicious attack on America.

So Saudi Arabia has two powerful forces cooperating together in its midst—money and religious fanaticism. The Saudis have a delicate balancing act of keeping the economic river flowing into their kingdom while at the same time appeasing fanatical Muslims who hate America and Israel with a passion. Which side will win is easy to see as it has been reported that the kingdom will run out of oil in the next fifty years. This seems unrealistic at first when we take into consideration that Saudi Arabia produces eight million barrels of oil a day. The Saudis also control one-fourth of the world's oil reserves. At our current oil usage rate, the reserves will run dry in a few decades, and Saudi Arabia will cease to be the world's biggest supplier. Religious fanaticism in Saudi Arabia, however, will never evaporate.

Saudi Minister of Interior Prince Nayef Ibn Abd-Al-Az said this when it comes to the tragic events of September 11, 2001, in New York and Washington, D.C.: "I think the Zionists are behind these events. It is impossible that 19 youths, including 15 Saudis, carried out the operation of September 11."[5] The prince went on to describe how he believes Zionist-controlled media in the United States manipulated the events and turned world opinion against Arabs and Islam.

I remember hearing about this fabricated story that was being circulated throughout the Middle East concerning the attack on America, and I seriously thought the Arabs would not believe it. How could they? The facts could not have been any clearer, and the motivation behind it was also well known. But while ministering in the Gaza Strip, I met people who believed it without question. Obviously, the terrorist strike was a major embarrassment to Muslims and especially to Saudi Arabia, the origin of most of the terrorists. So a public relations campaign was launched in the Muslim world to counter all negative publicity. What better group to hang the dirty deed on than the Jews! The roots of Islamic hatred toward Jews stem from Islam's very beginning in Saudi Arabia. In fact, because of how Islam was birthed, it will forever make despising Jews worldwide a positive virtue.

Down with Israel

When talking with Americans about the complexities of the Middle East situation, they eventually voice solutions that have to do with the superficials behind the problems. To many it seems that Israel should give the Palestinians a state. If only Israel would pull troops out of the West Bank. If only Israel would do this or that. It seems so easy—until you travel there and receive your personal crash course on Middle East religions. Herein lies the real problem. The wars, the intifadas, the suicide bombings, and the endless conflict have to do with religion more than politics.

In his excellent work *Islam and the Jews*, author Mark Gabriel chronicles why Islam and Judaism got off on the wrong foot. Although it seems impossible now, at one time Mecca and Medina each had a sizable Jewish population. Jewish merchants residing there filled Arab markets. Orthodox Jews lived out their faith for the most part without any serious problems. Arabs and Jews, the ancient cousins of the region, lived and worked side by side before Islam was established and Jews were forced out. Muhammad took the claims of the fledgling religion to Jews and Christians alike, believing that Islam was the logical fulfillment of both religions. He expected Jews to welcome him with open arms and embrace him as the latest in a very long line of prophets from

God. Jewish residents thoroughly rejected Muhammad and the new religion of Islam. They not only rejected him; they laughed at him. In early chapters of the Koran, Jews are respected and honored for their religious zeal and for being "people of the Book." But that changes suddenly in Islam's holy book as Allah supposedly gives Muhammad "further revelation" and proclaims judgment and condemnation on the Jews. At one point, they are even called "monkeys." When Osama bin Laden gave the hated Zionists this label, he was merely quoting from the Prophet Muhammad in the Koran, Surah (chapter) 7:166 and 5:60. Also in the Koran, Surah 2:65, Gabriel quotes, "And indeed you knew those amongst you [children of Israel] who transgressed in the matter of the Sabbath (i.e., Saturday). We said to them: 'Be you monkeys, despised and rejected.'" In his own words, Gabriel concludes that "Muslims interpret this to mean that Jews were literally turned into animals. But there is no information in the Quran (Koran) or in the Islamic history to answer the basic questions: (1) When did Allah transform Jews into monkeys and pigs? (2) Where did Allah transform Jews into monkeys and pigs? (3) Did Allah do that to the whole Jewish nation or just some of them? I never found any evidence that something like this happened to the Jewish people during their history. *The earlier revelations said the Jews were Allah's chosen people*" (Surah 2:47).[6]

Mark Gabriel earned a doctorate from the famed Al Azbar University in Cairo, Egypt. This is the most prestigious university for Islamic studies. Dr. Gabriel became a believer in the midst of teaching Islam at the university. He has since his conversion changed his name and moved out of the dangerous Middle East to the United States.

Not only does Islam have anti-Semitism as one of its core values; it also loathes the fact that Israel is back in the land and growing in all areas. To be fair, I have met numerous Muslims during my Middle East travels who do not hate Jews. Many of them see the issue differently from what one would expect. How can this be? Simple. As there are many Christians who do not take the Bible literally, so it is with Muslims. It is as easy for a Muslim to "spiritualize" his Koran as it is for a Christian to do so with his Bible. To some followers of Muhammad, the holy Koran is a historical account of the life and struggles of Islam. To others it is spiritual teaching, good for their souls. In short, if a Muslim fails to take the Koran at face value and believe it word for word, he may not show animosity toward Jews. Rather, the Muslim-Jewish struggle may be relegated to ancient tribal skirmishes that have no bearing on today's world. Unfortunately, Muslims who fall along these lines fail to ever be in any leadership positions. Leaders of the movement do take the Koran literally, and that is the reason no comprehensive peace will ever be forged in the region. To take away Jewish hatred would be to rob Islam of its soul. There will be land-for-peace attempts and peace treaties drawn up and redrawn. But the fundamental problem that Islam has with the Jews is their nagging existence. For Islam, it seems the Jews are here to stay. Recent statistics out of Israel report that Israel's population stands at 6.7 million people. The country's Jewish population is now 5.4 million. This is staggering for Muslims to comprehend that 38 percent of the world's Jewry now live in Israel.

Despite the current intifada, countless suicide bombings, and the daily threat of all-out war, the population grew 131,000 in Israel last year alone with more than 31,000 new immigrants. The campaign to intimidate Israelis and to discourage Jews from immigrating has backfired. Israel's population has grown more than eight times since it became a nation in 1948. People are flocking to Tel Aviv and to Jerusalem. They aren't flocking to Amman, Damascus, or Riyadh.

The War on Terrorism

In the last few years, as Americans, we have learned what it's like to be Jewish and to be living in the nation of Israel. With terrorism alerts and reports of fundamentalist Muslims roaming freely about America, our sense of security seems like something only experienced long ago. When President Bush correctly and courageously declared a war on terrorism, he drew a line in the sand that ultimately pitted America against Islam. The administration worked long and hard to differentiate between peaceful Muslims and hostile Muslims. The president even talked about how Muslim extremist terrorists had hijacked the religion. I believe the president is absolutely right. Sure the Koran glorified persecution of Jews and Christians. But most Muslims don't have any intention of fulfilling that call or of becoming terrorists. Most are no different from Americans who want to raise their children in peace, feed them well, and provide them with a good education. The majority of Muslims are truly peace-loving. Yet the leadership of the typical mosque continuously calls Allah's followers to join the battle and get in step with jihad so Islam can eventually take over the world. The messages are nonstop. To radical Muslims our war on terrorism is only a convenient excuse for America to keep Islam from spreading around the globe. It also is perceived as an excuse for us to unconditionally support Israel and its fight against Palestinians in Gaza and the West Bank.

It was right for America to liberate Iraq. The reign of the "Butcher of Baghdad" was one of the most evil periods in Middle East history. Saddam Hussein not only encouraged all-out war with America and Israel; he rewarded suicide bombers for killing innocent people all over Israel. The $25,000 helped inspire deceived Palestinian young people to blow themselves up and kill as many Jews as possible. The results of suicide bombings are as despicable as anything ever recorded in history. A disco filled with teenagers, families pushing baby strollers after attending evening worship, and shopping malls filled with women and children were all popular targets. Palestinian terrorist groups elevated suicide to a religious calling. Saddam Hussein personally wrote the big checks to families of the murderers. Even Adolf Hitler didn't think of this one!

Yet for all the American troops in the region, a major menace still exists that makes Iraq's evil empire pale in comparison. Syria is the military strongman of the area. Saudi Arabia has the money and the holy sites of Islam. Syria has the army, and the army is only miles away from Israel's famed Golan Heights, also known as Bashan from biblical days. David Dolan again underscored the serious threat of Israel's northern neighbor:

A new mideast war is almost inconceivable without Syrian participation. Damascus has an arsenal of weapons that nearly matches all of the other listed nations combined (Saudi Arabia, Jordan, Lebanon, Iraq, and the Palestinian Authority). Syria's standing army is estimated to be about three times the size of Israel's. Its tank and artillery forces, while substantially older than Israel's, are numerically much larger. In recent decades, Syria has acquired advanced warplanes and anti-aircraft missile systems from Moscow. But the main threat posed by Damascus is its substantial ballistic missile capability. Israel analysts estimate that the country can deploy up to one thousand independently targeted warheads. North Korean-built missiles have poured into Damascus airport; and the rogue Communist State has even licensed local production of Scud-L missiles, an improved version of the ones shot at Tel Aviv by Saddam Hussein. The prospect of such weapons striking Israeli targets is made more gruesome by the likelihood that they would carry chemical payloads. Syria is known to be producing VX nerve gas, one of the deadliest chemical agents on earth.[7]

Syria means business when it comes to dealing with Israel. Its military is ready and able, and its relationship is stronger than ever with Saudi Arabia.

In the end, I believe Syria's military prowess and Saudi Arabia's money and guardianship of Islamic religious cities will eventually join together in their efforts against Israel. Other Islamic nations will certainly have to follow along as the tidal wave movement to battle Israel. When Saudi Crown Prince Abdullah presented a peace proposal and an initiative to normalize relations with Israel, it was Syrian President Bashar Assad who pressed the Saudis to back down from the proposal. Assad himself arrived in Saudi Arabia in March of 2002 and pressed hard for fundamental changes that would keep the process from going any further. After the dictator's visit to Riyadh, the Saudis dropped the term "full normalization" of their relationship, and Syria's state-run news agency declared that Syria and Saudi Arabia had identical views on the matter. Saudi Arabia was clearly thinking about business growth around the world that would result with a softer treatment of Israel. Syria was thinking of maintaining the ongoing war of Islam versus Judaism. In the end, religion won out. In the Middle East, it always does. Syria and Saudi Arabia next time will probably move forward together when dealing with Israel. As the two nations team together, the Middle East and the world will feel the effects of their money, military, and religious fanaticism for the forces of Islam.

There is no question what prize radical Islam covets: Jerusalem. The Muslims lost it once to Christians. They lost it again to Jews. Islam demands control of Jerusalem. Muhammad taught that Judaism came first, Christianity came second, and now Islam is the fulfillment and culmination of the three great faiths. As a result, it is imperative for Islam to flex its muscle and to control the holy city of Jerusalem. The goal of Muslims to take Jerusalem is clear. It is the ultimate slap in the face that it is controlled now by Jews who supposedly have been passed over by God in favor of Islam, the new religion.

On the Horizon

What appears to be on the horizon? Dangerous alliances that are now being partnered together throughout the Islamic world. Alongside Syria and Saudi Arabia, Iran, which is non-Arab but Persian, is emerging with threatening rhetoric again. Northern Africa is almost exclusively Muslim now and has its own special brand of violent Islam. The ranks of Muslims are well spread globally. Here are some startling statistics: "Listed below are the fifty-three countries of the world that have at least 50 percent Muslim population or a Muslim plurality. The total population of these countries is more than 1 billion people or more than 78 percent of all the Muslims of the world. The countries are listed according to the actual size of their Muslim populations, *not* their total population."

Country	%	Population	Country	%	Population
Indonesia	80.3	165,550,000	Libya	96.5	5,018,000
Pakistan	96.1	139,316,000	Jordan	96.2	5,002,000
Bangladesh	85.6	114,316,000	Chad*	55.0	4,785,000
Turkey	99.6	66,061,000	Kyrgyzstan	78.1	3,904,000
Iran	99.0	65,452,000	Sierre Leone*	70.0	3,780,000
Egypt	86.5	60,391,000	Palestine	86.6	2,856,000
Nigeria*	41.0	51,906,000	Mauritania	99.8	2,696,000
Algeria	96.7	29,971,000	Lebanon	59.7	2,570,000
Morocco	99.9	29,156,000	Oman	92.7	2,224,000
Afghanistan	97.9	26,235,000	United Arab Emirates*	65.5	2,160,000
Iraq	96.9	22,857,000	Eritrea	47.9	2,063,000
Uzbekistan	83.5	20,959,000	Bosnia-Herzegovina*	60.1	2,042,000
Sudan	65.0	20,670,000	Kuwait	87.4	2,011,000
Saudi Arabia	92.8	19,587,000	Albania*	38.8	1,319,000
Yemen	99.9	17,989,000	Gambia	88.8	1,243,000

Country	%	Population	Country	%	Population
Syria	90.3	15,445,000	Burkina Faso	50.0	615,000
Malaysia	58.0	13,166,000	Comoros	98.1	588,000
Niger	97.6	10,149,000	Bahrain	82.3	576,000
Tunisia	99.7	9,667,000	Djibouti	93.9	563,000
Mali	87.0	9.570,000	Guinea-Bissau	43.0	516,000
Kazakstan*	60.5	8,954,000	Qatar	79.4	477,000
Senegal	92.1	8,931,000	Western		
			Sahara	100.0	300,000
Somalia	99.9	7,496,000	Maldives	99.4	298,000
Azerbaijan	83.7	6,777,000	Brunei	64.4	193,000
Guinea	85.4	5,549,000	Benin	20.0	132,000
Turkmenistan	91.8	5,051,000			

*Countries that have either a Muslim plurality or control of the government.[8]

These figures are from 2001 and have grown significantly since then. One-quarter of the world is now Muslim, approximately 1.3 billion people.

The sheer strength of numbers, influence, and wealth, along with the control of Arab culture and strong European Islamic backing, appears to be catastrophic for Israel in the future. Dangerous alliances worldwide are Muslim influenced, anti-Semitic, and contain the belief that one day Jerusalem will be taken out of Jewish hands altogether. A phrase being thrown around today is "international city," through which a group would seize control of Jerusalem and give it a United Nations form of government. But this would fail to appease Islam, which wants complete sovereignty in Jerusalem. In the future, I look for surrounding nations to enter a regional war for Jerusalem and Israel itself. How can Islam rest with Zionists in control of their "new" Holy City?

Chapter 5

Heroes of Our Faith

Despite the Middle East powder keg, the church is experiencing
an outpouring of God's power when it comes to salvation
among Arabs and Jews. Meet the believers who are the leaders
of this great revival. Their stories will inspire you with their
"live everyday as if it's the last one" mind-set.

The Globalization of Sin

In his best-selling book *Jihad vs. McWorld*, Benjamin Barber
wrote about democracy and its current global struggle with
terrorism. Despite his obvious distaste for the church, he made
a strong case for the reason Western culture is being rejected
in places where jihad is prized. "McWorld in tandem with the
global market economy has globalized many of our vices and
almost none of our virtues. We have globalized crime, the rogue
weapons trade, and drugs; we have globalized prostitution and
pornography, and the trade in women and children made by
porn tourism."[1]

His point is well taken. One thing Muslims and Christians
agree on is this: Western culture is depraved and decadent.
Certainly there is much good in our freedoms, yet the inherent
danger is that we will become a people of no restraint. Freedom
without personal restraint leads a culture into a spiritual free
fall. Barber quoted James Wolfensohn, president of the World
Bank, with these words: "Two billion people live on less than
two dollars a day. We live in a world that gradually is getting
worse and worse and worse. It is not hopeless, but we must do
something about it now."[2]

I agree that our world has entered into a new period of desperation. Poverty is on the rise. More wars are on the horizon. Terrorism is just getting started. Money will not solve our problems. Globalization will not solve our problems. Democracy will set people groups free, but it is the church that must pick up the slack and deal with the spiritual vacuum left once an evil regime is removed. Iraq cries out for revival not for Western culture. Democracy is a blessing to any nation. But if the church is not strong, vibrant, and able to influence within the democracy, heathenism will likely result.

The Church Is the Answer

How disturbing it was to watch CNN when Afghanistan was being liberated from Taliban rule. I was thrilled to see that a certain amount of religious reform would now be allowed. Good! The fear gripping millions of Afghans that is always a by-product of fundamentalist Islam was receding. This also was good. Women would no longer be squelched and would now be free to receive an education. Another good thing. American soldiers entered into an extremely difficult war and served faithfully and valiantly with effectiveness. Osama bin Laden may have eluded our special forces in the endless caves of Afghanistan, but since he was on the run, he was marginalized. America has not been attacked by him directly since. All of these things are good.

What disturbed me was to watch CNN broadcast videotape to the world of Afghan men holding *Playboy* magazines up to the cameras with big smiles. My heart sank! After all, that was what Muslims of the Middle East say we Americans are all about anyway. We are portrayed as a nation of addicts— addicted to pornography, alcohol, overeating, immorality, and violence. Where in the world would Afghans get an idea like that? By what they see and hear in American movies and television. Our culture is infamous worldwide. Our personal excesses and our extremism are what we are known for globally. America is a fast-growing mission field. What Afghanistan needs is a big dose of Jesus. Western culture will leave Afghans feeling as empty as they were before. Maybe their lifestyle will improve, but without Christ they will still die in their sin and go straight to hell. Jesus' message of real freedom is what is needed in a hurry. The pure gospel that sets us free from our personal sin will revolutionize Afghanistan. McDonald's will not. Don't get me wrong. I love a Big Mac, but the church has all the answers. Western culture without Jesus Christ right in the middle of it will not deliver what it promises. Americans can testify to this. So can Israel.

A Wrong Turn for Israel

Israel is an amazing nation in many ways. Becoming a state recognized by the United Nations in 1948 presented Jews and Arabs with a unique set of problems. Jews from Eastern Europe and Russia were used to a communist form of government. Some of these tenets were adopted into kibbutz life throughout Israel. Jewish families together bought land and farmed it. The kibbutzim of Israel were small villages that provided a certain amount of protection to its many residents. The profits were split evenly no matter the job or the production level, just as they had been in the Soviet Union. Israel would certainly not adopt communism as a form of national government, would it? Apparently the Soviet Union thought it might and actually voted for Israel's reconstitution as a nation in the 1947 United Nations vote.

At the other end of the spectrum were Orthodox Jews from many countries who longed to return to Israel's form of government they enjoyed in Old Testament days. Before Israel demanded a king as the other nations had, it was a theocracy—literally, a nation "ruled by God." Unfortunately, Israel wanted a monarchial system, which would provide the Hebrews with a king. Their leaders previously were prophets and judges Yahweh handpicked to serve directly under Him. Israel wanted to redo its system of government, and it ended up being the colossal failure of the Old Testament. The prophet Samuel's sons did not walk after God as Samuel did, and the spiritual void left the leaders of God's nation feeling insecure and vulnerable.

Recorded in 1 Samuel 8:4–7 is their reasoning: "So all the elders of Israel gathered together and went to Samuel at Ramah. They said to him, 'Look, you are old, and your sons do not follow your example. Therefore, appoint a king to judge us the same as all the other nations have.' When they said, 'Give us a king to judge us,' Samuel considered their demand sinful, so he prayed to the LORD. But the LORD told him, 'Listen to the people and everything they say to you. They have rejected you; they have rejected Me as their king.'" Of course, this ended up being what made Israel unravel at the seams and fall apart completely.

To be sure, there were some high points with King Solomon and his father King David, but the model was all wrong to begin with. Borrowed from the surrounding pagan nations, this form of government was doomed from the beginning. God had laid out clear rules and responsibilities in the Pentateuch along with spiritual ones, and He was quite capable of managing His holy nation Himself, thank you very much! Yet God granted the Israelite request, and Israel never recovered. Orthodox Jews in Israel certainly didn't want to repeat that error again. They desired a theocracy—the only pure form of government.

As it turned out, Israel opted to become a democratic republic like America, which backed the new nation throughout the whole process. This form of government was replete with voting privileges, freedom of religion, and a free enterprise system that soared upon takeoff. Freedoms were new for many of their residents. For Arabs, they were no longer under Turkish Ottoman rule. Also, the British mandate period was over, and Arabs who became citizens of Israel finally lived within the boundaries of a free society. In Nazareth, a friend of mine whose family has lived in Jesus' hometown for a few centuries sings the praises of how his life and very existence changed for the good when Israel was reestablished in the land.

For Jews, freedom was just as sweet! Fresh from Nazi death camps and European oppression, Jews were finally free. No wonder early films of Israeli citizens so often showed them dancing in a circle with joy! Everyone had rights, and Jews would no longer be under cruel dictatorships they had been subject to in the past. There was good—so much good.

Just as with other democracies of the world, when the church is weak and ineffective, there is great potential for problems. Israel was enjoying life within the world of the free. The church, however, was traditional in form and for the most part devoid of anyone having a born-again experience. Jerusalem, the birthplace of Jesus' church, was a far cry from first-century days when the apostle Peter spoke to the masses at Solomon's Colonnade, and five thousand Jews were saved. However, once Israel became a nation again, salvation experiences were almost nonexistent. One longtime Jerusalem resident who moved to the city in 1960 remembers only four believers in all of Israel that he knew of. Lots of religion—not much Jesus.

Over the years, religion grew in Israel. Since it was for the most part without Jesus, so did worldliness. Religion can never fend off worldliness. Only Jesus living and residing in people's lives and hearts will turn a culture away from the false claims of the world and toward God Himself. Israel would have been a miracle by just hanging on after each decade's major war. The Israelis not only hung on; they prospered. They became world leaders in medicine, technology, and agriculture. God's hand of blessing clearly was guiding the nation once again.

The church, however, was miniscule. Over time, Israel has gotten caught up in worldliness that is shocking to see on one's arrival in Tel Aviv. The city named the "hill of the spring" prides itself in its modernity and liberal nature. It's like a San Francisco in the Holy Land. If Jerusalem is the old holy city, then Tel Aviv is the new secular city. The place where David Ben-Gurion read opening words to the new nation of Israel recently was voted the "Gay Capital of the World." Somehow it's hard to believe that this is what the nation's forefathers had in mind during the rebirth of Israel in May of 1948.

It also is interesting to note the rise of Kabbala, which is the current rage in Israel and throughout the world. Kabbala is sort of a New Age form of Judaism, and its capital city, Safed, Israel, is just north of the Sea of Galilee. With heavy marketing and superstar appeal, Kabbala is Judaism without all the confining rules. Terms like "negative energy," "creative guidance," and "rays of light" permeate the hip, growing Hebrew splinter group. Madonna, Barbra Streisand, Jeff Goldblum, Mick Jagger, Elton John, Demi Moore, and Elizabeth Taylor have all turned to Kabbala.

Today, Israel is still free. Jews are free! So are Arabs who become citizens of the state of Israel. Democracy and freedom are blessings that stand out in the midst of oppressive dictatorships all around. But freedom without the restraining power of the Holy Spirit is resulting in a wave of modern iniquity. Israel finds itself wanting to be like other nations again, primarily in the West, that are rapidly turning away from God.

Just Say No to Jesus

In Colorado Springs there are about 150 ministry headquarters within the city. Some of the most notable are

Compassion International, International Bible Society, Focus on the Family, and the Navigators. With many ministries in town, the area is often in the midst of Christian initiatives sweeping the country. One of these campaigns was the WWJD movement. Youth all over the United States were wearing wristbands with the letters WWJD, which stood for "What Would Jesus Do?" It was a physical reminder for believers to live as Jesus would have in any situation. Well, Colorado Springs was knee-deep in WWJD bracelets. They were all over the place! One day a young girl was wearing her bracelet, and she encountered some resistance from a group of young people known within school as Satan worshippers. Unfortunately, they, too, are in Colorado Springs. One of the rough-looking kids approached her in a crowded hall and said, "I like your WWJD bracelet. I think it's cool." He baited her. "I wear mine upside down. It means to me 'We want Jesus dead!'" The hall fell silent as the sweet young Christian replied very calmly, "We want Jesus dead, huh?" "Yeah," he said. With a burst of confidence, she said, "Well, they already tried that once, and it didn't work!" The hall full of kids laughed hard as the pure facts of the gospel quite nicely turned back his arrogance.

So it is in Israel. Pictures of Jesus are everywhere—often pictured on the cross. That's where many people want Him to stay. Jesus still makes as many waves in Jerusalem as He did two thousand years ago. There is not much difference. In fact, Israel's unofficial "Just Say No to Jesus" campaign in the last few years has been evident in a variety of places. Here are some of the places the campaign to squelch Jesus has been found:

In the Political Realm

During Prime Minister Netanyahu's administration, Orthodox rabbis pushed a bill all the way to the Knesset that would have forbidden all forms of evangelism within Israel. This was obviously aimed straight at Christian evangelicals. It was perceived in America as a big slap in the face to Christians who are for the most part supportive of Israel. The antimissionary law in Israel was ultimately too difficult to pass. Since Israel is a democracy, this would have clearly cut at the right to religious freedom. Benjamin Netanyahu's office was besieged with protest faxes mainly from America. This shows how sensitive the issue of conversion is in Israel. It is so hot that some wanted the nation to undo some of its core values in order to put an end to it. Thankfully, the resolution failed.

On Television

Two years ago, an important television program aired live in Israel. Gathered in the studio were religious leaders from every spectrum of Judaism. The topic was "What is a Jew?" Various spokesmen each had their allotted time, and they waxed eloquent about their respective movements within Judaism. Orthodox, Conservative, and Reformed Jews all spoke with passion about their slice of the ancient religion. Also, there were atheistic Hebrews present at the television show. They were environmentalists who worshipped nature and found no room in their theology for a personal God whatsoever. Messianic believers were also present. The religious groups represented were quite diverse.

At the end of the program, "What is a Jew?" was answered finally, and the conclusions drawn were predictable. A Jew could come in all sorts of flavors. Judaism in various forms from Orthodox to atheistic was acceptable for Jews of Israel. You could take the *Tanach* (Old Testament) literally and be a good Jew, or you could not take it literally and be a tree hugger, for instance, and be a good Jew. The only thing that disqualified you whatsoever from Hebraic roots was believing that Jesus was Messiah. In other words, if you were a messianic Jew, you were no longer considered Jewish. Despite the protest of the messianic participant, the entire panel agreed with this conclusion. Judaism had no room for followers of Yeshua. Amazing! Atheists were welcome. Messianics were not.

In the News

About four years ago the *Jerusalem Post* ran an article, "The Problem of Messianic Judaism." The column talked about Jews converting to Christianity in Israel. They considered this a real threat. More Jews had converted to Christianity in the last nineteen years than in the last nineteen centuries. The Orthodox rabbinate was concerned about the thinning ranks of traditional Judaism. The leaders were now offering a seminar on how to defeat the claims of Christianity and its supposed negative effects on Jewish culture. No wonder Jesus wept over Jerusalem! The negative effects on Jewish culture? Jesus is the fulfillment of the Abrahamic covenant that will bring blessing to all the nations. It was amazing to me that messianics were considered dangerous. After all, this is the country that is stocked with terrorists and plenty of suicide bombers.

A New Work of the Spirit

In no way can the miracle of Israel's return to the land, preservation in the land, and prosperity in the land be minimized. The hostility encircling Israel could be all-consuming. Yet, Israel continues to develop and soar to new heights economically. Lifestyles are good in Israel. There is absolutely no comparison anywhere in the region. God's covenant to bless Israel is the only way to explain all of this. In our lifetime, we have witnessed a miracle that is on par with any act of God in Old Testament days.

Yet, the people thirst for a personal work of God in their hearts. In the past few years while visiting Israel, I have seen openness like never before. Jews and Arabs are finding Jesus. It appears that God is using the three-year intifada to bring about a mood of desperation. Both groups of people are wrestling with the endless struggle and searching for some kind of hope. The operative word here is *desperation*. God works in desperation. God moves in the midst of it. It is fertile ground for the gospel. It is the best spiritual climate for the church to advance in.

In a recent worship service in Tel Aviv, the messianic pastor spoke of the fear pervading the city. Suicide bombers were dressing up as Hasidic Jews and infiltrating heavily populated Jewish areas before detonating their bombs. Women were now blowing themselves up. The attacks were steady, deadly, and devastating. The mood of the normally upbeat youth was understandably oppressive and gloomy. People avoided coffee shops and clubs. Terrorism was winning as people's lives were severely affected.

The spiritual leader asked for a show of hands to a revealing question: "How many of you have had a relative or a close friend involved in a suicide bombing?" With great sadness, every hand went up. It was a clean sweep. Terrorism had affected every Tel Aviv resident within the church. The pastor skillfully reminded the believers of God's words written by King David in Psalm 27:1: "The LORD is my light and my salvation—whom should I fear? The LORD is the stronghold of my life—of whom should I be afraid?" The words couldn't have been more timely. These Israelis live in a country where no place is safe because schools, city buses, synagogues, and holy sites are often targeted. Yet, God is using all of the pain to drive His people back to Him. The body of believers in Israel is growing faster than ever.

Today, in Israel there are between 120 and 200 messianic

convocations. The promulgation of the gospel has been slow among Israelis for decades, but it appears the spiritual logjam is now breaking up. In a new magazine called *Kivun*, which means "direction" in Hebrew, messianics are finding connection, and the growth of the movement is impressive. The first issue of *Kivun* said:

> Gone are the days when Israeli Messianic Jews were a small secluded group. The changes in recent years have created the need for a Hebrew language magazine that meets the unique needs of its readership. Not the least of these changes is the impressive growth in the number of Messianic Jews, especially over the past two decades. We're not speaking of a few dozen here and there, but of thousands who express their loyalty to the God of Israel by their lifestyle. The increase in numbers has birthed a heightened sense of confidence on both an individual and congregational level. This confidence translates to a growing willingness to be exposed to the general public, an exposure dictated by reality and consistent with the philosophy of Messianic Judaism.[3]

What a big step forward for messianic believers. Formerly, if a Jew accepted Jesus as the Jewish Messiah, the temptation was to keep it as quiet as possible. Jobs were lost, families were ripped apart, and public scorn was intense whenever a Jew "defected" to Christianity. Nothing could have been considered worse for a Jew than embracing Jesus as Messiah within the borders of Israel.

The church that Jesus founded in Israel was one with power, abounding grace, and contagious love. Yet over the centuries the bride of Christ had become weak and institutionalized. Life was missing in the very place where Jesus conquered death. But that life has returned! Only a few years ago there were four messianic congregations, and now there are sixty—sixty life-giving congregations bring living water to the spiritually thirsty.

Creative Evangelism

Outreach to Jews in Israel can be tricky. Residents are very familiar with what we Christians believe and what the New Testament says about Jesus, the Jewish Messiah. The apostle Paul experienced a burden in his heart for his Jewish brethren. His emotional outpouring about Jewish outreach is detailed masterfully in Romans 9–11. As the apostle began, his heart was breaking for his Jewish kinsmen who are separated from Christ. In Romans 9:3, he said, "For I could wish that I myself were cursed and cut off from the Messiah for the benefit of my brothers, my countrymen by physical descent." He was saying, "If I could take their place and go to hell on their behalf, I would do it." Powerful words. The height of sacrifice.

So it is with those who labor with Jewish lost people. They are so close, but through their own heart's hardness, they are missing out on the pinnacle of their spiritual heritage. Paul rolled out their vast spiritual wealth in verses 4 and 5: "They are Israelites, and to them belong the adoption, the glory, the covenants, the giving of the law, the temple service, and the promises. The forefathers are theirs, and from them, by physical descent, came the Messiah, who is God over all, blessed forever. Amen."

Jews, God's chosen people, could not have been more spiritually advantaged. God's revelation. God's spokesmen. God's miracles. All of these are forever contained in their spiritual history. That's why it's so heartbreaking. The missing centerpiece of their spiritual puzzle is right before their eyes. Yet now Jewish eyes are beginning to open. Let's look at recent examples of this.

A Bombed-out Shop

In Jerusalem after a suicide bombing last year on Ben Yehuda Street, an American tour group decided to get involved. A pastor and several parishioners went to pray at the site of the attack on innocent Jewish lives. As they were walking through the area, they spotted a Jewish man sitting in his souvenir shop. Since it was close to where the bomb was exploded, the man's shop was in shambles. He sat in a chair and wept. The pastor, sensing the man desperately needed an encouraging friend, entered the shop that was a burned disaster area. He asked, "Could I please buy a menorah?" The man never looked up but said, "Fifty percent off." The pastor said, "I don't want to buy it for 50 percent off." The shopkeeper said, "OK, 60 percent off." The wise minister shocked the Jewish merchant by saying, "I want to pay full price!" The rest of the group then lined up behind the pastor and likewise each bought a Jewish lamp stand at full price. It was an amazing gesture. No one pays full price in Israel. It is the Middle East home for "let's make a deal!" Moved by their goodwill, the elderly Jewish man asked, "Who are you?" The pastor told the man that they were Christians from America, and they were visiting to show their solidarity with Israel. The old shop owner went on to tell the group that it was Christians from America who were keeping the Israeli economy from collapsing. He said Christians were coming to Israel in the midst of the intifada, and that was amazing to him since Jews were no longer visiting. Hardly any Jewish bar mitzvahs were being done any longer at Jerusalem's Western Wall. But Christians were still arriving daily. The man said to the group, "Tell me about Jesus again. Maybe I need to give Him a second look."

The apostle Paul would have been smiling. Now that is the way to reach out to Abraham's descendants! We cannot give them anymore information. They have heard it all before. But they can be reached by our love. They resent Christian know-it-alls, but they are moved by humility. They are touched by our friendship. Put yourself in Jewish shoes for a minute. They are surrounded by enemies everywhere they look. Imagine the impact of only one group consistently reaching out to them with genuine love in their hearts. The Christians. I believe Jesus is calling His church to step forward right now and love Israel back to Him. We can do it. We must!

An Orthodox Rabbi's Son

Traditional Orthodox Judaism is struggling to reach today's generation. Orthodox parents have a battle on their hands with the overt worldliness that is so prevalent in the land. Since Judaism is steeped in legalism, it often is a real turnoff with the young people of Israel. In some ways, the traditionally garbed Jews are seen as outdated and irrelevant. Like the Amish of Lancaster, Pennsylvania, the Orthodox Jews stand out in modern Israel. Many families have lost their young people to the enticements of the world.

At the Dugit Coffee Shop of Tel Aviv, an Orthodox rabbi's young son was disenchanted with religion. Avi engaged him in a conversation and asked the man why he hadn't considered Jesus in his life search. The young man was unfamiliar with any evidence from Scripture, so Avi gladly gave him prophetical verses about the Messiah from the Old Testament. After a week or so, he returned for a cup of coffee. He said he thought Jesus might be the Messiah spoken about by the prophets of Israel. Avi pressed further. "What would Jesus have to do to prove to you that He is the Messiah?" The young man without hesitation said, "If Jesus could get me a job, I'd believe He was the Messiah. I haven't had one in about six months." Avi never missed a beat. "Let's pray that he does that for you!" Avi put his arm around the man and prayed a prayer of faith, "Lord, Jesus, show this young man that you alone are God and that you want to save him from his sins. Please get him a job, Lord Jesus!" As they were praying, the man's cell phone began to ring. He looked at Avi, and his Jewish face turned white. He answered the phone, and he was offered a job right then and there. The job started the next day! Avi reminded him of his challenge to Jesus and that He had more than met that challenge. Now it was up to him. The Orthodox rabbi's son lowered his head and received Jesus Christ as his Messiah.

As you can imagine, this set off a spiritual bomb at his parents' house, and they ceased all contact and communication with him. They said their son had died. His new church family welcomed him with open arms, and he is walking with Jesus Christ, his Savior. God loves to answer prayers of faith like that.

Hospital and Rehab Outreach

Zeke and Carrie Bristol had a dream to start a different type of ministry in Israel. As the tragedies mounted, they decided to do something. People were being killed throughout Israel by suicide bombers on a regular basis. The numbers of the wounded in the attacks were staggering. These people were often overlooked. In May of 2003, the intifada was thirty months old, and 5,157 people had already been wounded. Almost nightly on the news the body count grows. The wounded will never be the same, and many of them will stay in a hospital or a rehabilitation center for the rest of their lives.

The Bristols, along with other local believers, host a weekly event at a rehab center. Patients stream into the cafeteria every Thursday night, some in wheelchairs and others in hospital beds. They are greeted with soft drinks, chips, and lots of desserts. A messianic group sings praise songs, and believers mingle with the patients. The mood is light and happy, and everyone is having a great time. While we visited the party, the best part was definitely the wheelchair dancing. The people go away knowing they are loved and not forgotten. This is practical outreach at its best. Jesus reached out to the sick and the hurting and prayed for them. His church is following His lead and doing the same for the neediest people of the land today.

Jewish outreach is being carried out by messianic believers and dynamic churches all throughout Israel. A few years ago, there was only a handful of churches reaching their Jewish brethren for Christ. Now there are between 120 and 200. There are several effective parachurch groups as well. The gospel is moving freely throughout Israel once again.

The Cross versus the Crescent Moon

The news from Palestinian areas and among Israeli Arabs is even better. Arab churches are growing rapidly, and their goal to reach Muslims and nominal Christians is contagious. Caught in between Muslims and Jews, the Arab church is in one of the most difficult situations anywhere in the world. These dynamic believers operate on the front lines of the Arab-Israeli ongoing conflict. They often are caught in the middle. The situation in the Gaza Strip and in the West Bank is deplorable. Refugee camps have housed frustrated Palestinians for fifty-six years now.

At this point, I must clarify a few things. My heart goes out to Arabs in Israel, especially Palestinians. So far we have looked at Israel's history and the great moving of God to preserve the Jews in this hostile land. I believe it is Israel's historical and biblical right to possess the land. When I shared this on a radio program this year, a local caller accused me of hating Palestinians. I said, "Absolutely not!" Ninety percent of our ministry right now is with Arab believers. We love them, and my wife and I are drawn to the Arab culture. They are the most hospitable people we have ever met!

But we are talking about two different issues here. Israel has a right to the land, and Israelis have proven over the decades that they are willing to share it with the Palestinians. Most Palestinians want peace with Israel. Often Palestinian leadership has proven that it does not. The Palestinians are forced to minister within a cauldron of hate. The Palestinian church leadership is top-notch. The pastors are some of the finest, most dedicated, humble servants of God anywhere.

The Gaza Miracle

Brother Andrew is one of my heroes. He is the Christian version of Indiana Jones. His exploits for the kingdom of God are legendary. In his 1996 book *The Calling*, Andrew talked about the Muslim world as the final frontier for the gospel. Like most of us, he was surprised to hear of kingdom expansion occurring in the midst of Middle East Islam. The work being done by Jesus' church is remarkable. Andrew correctly drew the battle lines for us. "I have come to believe that Islam possesses the biggest challenge to the church today. Not to political or economic systems but to the church. Why? Quite simply, because we in the western church don't come close to matching the level of commitment, determination, and strength of many Muslim groups. Christ and the Bible certainly call us to radical commitment, but we don't show it in the way we live. Until we do, Islam will continue to be the world's fastest growing religion—not because of its strength but because of our weakness."[4]

Exactly, Andrew. C'mon, church—wake up! We have the words of life. We must not only match their commitment level; we must exceed it. Signs of the church waking up are all around us. The September 11 attack on America put all the

Islamic cards on the table. In the past few years the church has shifted into a higher gear. The momentum is changing.

Andrew went on to talk about the neediest areas throughout the Muslim world. He mentioned the church in the Gaza Strip was without a pastor for many years. As I read about the struggling church, I was surprised to hear of a church in the Gaza Strip. I'd been going to Israel for some time and had no idea there was a church in Gaza. How could there be? Radical terrorist groups roam freely here. Islamic Jihad, Hamas, and the Al-Aksa Martyrs Brigade all have home bases here. The Gaza Strip is seven miles wide and twenty-six miles long. It is the most densely populated area in the world. It is home to about 1.5 million people, and 99.9 percent of these are Muslims. Hardly a night goes by that Gaza is not in the news. When you enter Gaza, you are officially in the trenches.

A few years ago the only evangelical church in the Gaza Strip did get a pastor. Ibraham (name changed for his protection) is God's man for Gaza. The church has gone from a handful of members to about three hundred since Ibraham arrived. The pastor now disciples a group of young men who will be the future leaders of the Gaza church. The believers of the church are empowered by the Holy Spirit and are fearless. They distribute food in the refugee camps. They give Bibles to all who are interested. They reach out to Muslims. The church is alive. What impresses me about the Gaza believers is that they show no traces of bitterness despite their impossible political situation. Gaza has a long and unsettling history. In the Old Testament this was Philistine country and home to one of Israel's archenemies. This spiritual stronghold is permeated with oppression. When conflict breaks out, the Erez crossing closes, and Palestinians are kept from their jobs in Israel due to security breaches. All of this contributes to an oppressive feeling always present in Gaza. Gunfire is heard daily. There is violence in the air.

Christ is being lifted up in the Gaza Strip, and, one by one, Muslims are being reached for Jesus. What attracts them to Christ is the fruit of the Spirit on display through the believers' lives. The church's abundant joy is infectious. Muslims and nominal Christians notice a difference. Jesus is alive in Gaza. Signs of war are all around, but you would never know it when you enter the believers' homes. The difference is truly night from day.

A children's club recently began in the church. Ironically, as I wrote this, Gaza was hit by several missile strikes after a terrorist bus bombing in Jerusalem. The news showed it live, and it was relatively close to the church. I called Pastor Ibraham to check and see if everyone was all right. He was unaware of the missiles because about one hundred kids were in the church hooting and hollering during Awana game time. They were oblivious to the danger all around them. Gaza outside was now rioting. Inside the church, the children were completely sheltered and memorizing their Bible verses for the week.

The gospel is liberating peoples from their chains in the Gaza Strip. The church, although harassed, persecuted, and in constant danger, is unmoved by the overwhelming odds against it. The believers' vision to reach the Strip and their passion for souls are going to be rewarded at the judgment seat of Christ one day. Unless you go to Gaza, you will be unfamiliar with their names until heaven. They are warriors for Christ. Their rewards await them, and their crowns are ready.

Jordan—Launching Pad for Arab Outreach

Pastor Aziz had a startling experience. A Muslim man who lived across the street was on to the pastor. The ornery neighbor informed the seasoned man of God that if he talked to him about Jesus he would order his murder. Since the pastor had been arrested several times, this was nothing new to him. He was quite used to persecution by now. His wife summarized their existence with words I will remember for life: "Most of the leaders of our church have been arrested by the authorities at least once. But I think every Christian should be arrested for their faith at least once in their life because after being arrested your fear leaves you." What penetrating words those were to my soul! Would I be willing to be arrested for Christ?

After September 11, 2001, Pastor Aziz was in an Amman, Jordan, outdoor market. The man who had threatened him earlier called out to him loudly across from the fruit stand. The pastor was surprised as the formerly surly acquaintance told him of his new spiritual search. "I'm sick of Islam," he blurted out. "It is consumed with violence and world domination, and I've had it!" Aziz asked the man if he could visit with him about Jesus. He said, "Let's talk soon. But until then, when your church sings, please leave your windows open because those songs speak to my heart."

This man's about-face is a window into the religion of Islam today. Many followers of Muhammad are privately questioning their religion and its real motives. Missionaries in the Middle East are saying that Muslims have not been this open to the saving grace of Jesus Christ for thirteen centuries. The Jordanian pastor explained in this way: "September 11 was a terrible tragedy not just for America but for the world. If you track Islam worldwide, you will be able to find it quickly because it leaves a trace of blood in its path. But the lives that were lost on September 11 were not lost in vain because it triggered a revival among Muslims. Their religion has been exposed, and they have many questions to be answered. We believe Jesus has the answers to their questions."

The Amman church began an Internet chat room outreach program nightly. The "hits" were so numerous that the church had to go from one computer to three, then to five. Next, it moved up to nine computers. The volume continued to rise.

The church has just purchased its fifteenth computer. Every night trained leaders from the church engage Muslims in chat rooms and in a safe atmosphere answer their questions about Jesus. Nightly, lives are rescued from the darkness of Islam and delivered safely into the loving arms of Jesus. Through Internet evangelism, people are having an online born-again experience in closed Islamic countries—Libya, Saudi Arabia, Iran, Egypt, Syria, and many more. The church follows up the babes in Christ with solid discipleship materials. When someone places his trust in Christ and forsakes Islam, a thumb goes up from the happy gospel sharer. Every night several thumbs-up are seen.

The holy fire is spreading throughout Jordan. Jesus films and thousands of EvangeCubes are now in the country. Believers are serious about sharing Christ and being His Jordanian ambassadors. The Jordan Evangelical Theological Seminary trains more than one hundred students per year. The Middle East's only evangelical seminary cannot enroll all the students interested. The ministries are well connected and focused on the vast needs of the region. The believers planted ten Iraqi churches throughout Jordan after the first Gulf War because many Iraqi refugees came into the Hashemite kingdom (Jordan) as a result of Desert Storm. The churches sensed a big open door and led many to Christ. The Iraqis continue to hope for a return to their country one day. The day has arrived, and believers have returned to Iraq to help stabilize the church there and to begin a countrywide church-planting initiative. Pastor Aziz recently called me to say that he was in Baghdad, helping to equip the church. An American soldier preached the sermon in the worship service, and Aziz trained believers to share their faith with the EvangeCube. It doesn't get any better than this.

The Jordanian church and its dynamic pastor are the influencers of the region. They train, shepherd, and help resource pastors in Gaza, the West Bank, and in all Arab countries.

One believer is a teacher in a private Christian school. Since public schools are often lacking, many Muslim families go to private schools even if they are Christian-based. The teacher shared the EvangeCube with one class and led forty young people to the Lord! He is systematically working his way through the school.

And Their Young Men Will Dream Dreams

The prophet Joel talked about a prophetic outpouring that would bless the nation of Israel during the coming of the Lord. Visions, dreams, and a spectacular display of God's power would accompany this golden age. In the past ten years, missionaries have continually heard of a similar phenomenon in the Muslim world. People began having dreams. Others started having visions. Jesus is manifesting Himself to devout Muslims with overwhelming power. I have personally met several of these people. Their stories amaze me as I see the depth of God's pursuing love. Paul said to Timothy in his pastoral Epistle to the young leader that God "wants everyone to be saved and to come to the knowledge of the truth" (1 Tim. 2:4). In other words, the heart of God cries out for a full house in heaven. Yet in many areas the Gospel is not available for all who hunger. Nowhere is this seen more than behind the spiritual iron curtain of Islam. What's a fair God to do? God often does the unexpected. The spectacular. He sends visions and dreams. God goes extreme.

We've met them. A man who saw Jesus calling him and saying, "Forsake Allah and come to Me." A woman praying to Allah, and when she opened her eyes a vision of Jesus was unfolding before her. Since Muslims have Jesus in their "system" and are familiar with Him, this helps break down any barriers that they might have with Christians in general. True, Islam teaches that Jesus is only a prophet, but when He appears with such power, they are convinced. Jesus has revealed Himself in Mecca, Baghdad, Damascus, Tehran—some of the most restricted Islamic cities. Because of His wonderful, long-suffering patience with this sin-infested world, He is not willing to give up on the people who follow Muhammad. He wants to reach them like anyone else—and He is.

The Arab church is advancing God's kingdom into the inner recesses of Islam. The messianic church is clearly on the move too. God is supplying His power abundantly. Pastors like Avi, Ibraham, and Aziz are filled to overflowing with the Holy Spirit, and the church is growing. Jews are converting; Muslims are too. Is there any hope of seeing genuine reconciliation between the two sons of Abraham? We'll cover the answer to that question in chapter 7, "The Mission Heart of God."

★ ☼ ★ ☼

Jamal—Son of Thunder

JAMAL IS A WORK OF ART. This Arab believer is a ball of fire if there ever was one. His sense of humor is nonstop. He has an infectious smile. He loves Jesus with all of his "heart, soul, and strength." He is one of those rare people in life who uses laughter like a spiritual gift. In the midst of danger, threats, and constant scrutiny, Jamal's smile is always present. He has been aptly described as an Arabic version of Jonathan Winters, the comedic "teddy bear" of the sixties and seventies. When Jamal is holding court, the jokes are clean and really funny. Then he turns to spiritual issues, and his wisdom and experience begin to pour out.

Jamal is a veteran of the spiritual war in the Middle East throughout his life. He lives in the trenches. He fights the good fight that is all around him. He knows all the right people throughout the Arabic world. He shared the gospel with Yasser

Arafat once. Onlookers say the Palestinian chairman had tears in his eyes as Jamal shared with him. Jamal has also told Jordanian officials all about Christ and his life-transforming ability. He backs down to no one. That component doesn't fit within his spiritual nature.

In life there are people who are thoroughly committed to Christ and accomplish much for Him. Jamal is that and more. He is not only a high-achiever but an influencer as well. To spend time with Jamal means that at the end of the day one will do a spiritual self-examination. It naturally happens while ministering with him. Christian leaders of the region look up to him. He achieves much for the kingdom of God and influences so many in the region. For the Middle East world, he's perfect. He often says, "If you want to serve Jesus faithfully in the Middle East, you must be a little crazy!"

Jamal grew up in Nazareth, an Israeli/Arab town. Much different from the desperate state that other Palestinians find themselves in, Nazareth's Arab citizens have a solidly middle-to-upper middle-class living situation. Since they chose to accept Israel and also accepted citizenship, they hardly resemble their Palestinian relatives who struggle to survive. Most Arabs of Nazareth have good jobs and find themselves isolated from the ongoing conflict that blazes only a few miles away in the West Bank.

God began to burden Jamal for the lost in Jordan. So many Muslims thought that they knew what Christianity was all about. Yet their prejudice against Jesus and the Bible stemmed from the erroneous presentation of them by Muslim leaders. Islamic apologue is its claim that:

- Christians worship three Gods.
- Jews corrupted the Old Testament.
- Jews hate Muslims because they themselves have been rejected by God, and Muslims have been accepted by God.
- Miriam, Moses' sister, was the mother of Jesus.

- Jesus did not rise from the dead.
- Jesus will convert to Islam.
- Christians took prophecies of Muhammad out of the New Testament.

Jamal, though comfortable in Nazareth, wanted to join the battle, and he enlisted to be on the front lines. Jordan is the gateway to the world of Islam. It is respected by other Muslim countries. The king is supposedly a descendant of Muhammad. It borders three strategic Islamic nations—Syria to the north, Iraq to the east, and Saudi Arabia to the south. On the western side is Israel. Jordan is definitely placed in the heart of the conflict. This is a hub for evangelism among Muslims. With Jordan's relatively easy access into surrounding countries, Jamal is able to travel freely and encourage believers in ministry all around the Middle East. He gives of himself tirelessly and often gets only four hours of sleep a night, his wife says.

Since Jamal lives on the edge and encourages others to do so, he has been arrested many times and so has his leadership team. He is hauled in for questioning. He is followed. He knows at all church services there are "listening ears." Jamal has written ninety Iraqi praise songs. Ninety! They are beautiful expressions of praise and worship to the God who is over all, even Jordan.

More than one Christian leader has told me that Jamal is a hero for Jesus Christ in the Middle East. Jamal is intense, yet lighthearted all at the same time. He is a regional leader for a parachurch ministry with forty staff members under him. He pastors a church. He leads evangelistic campaigns. He disciples many men. He has a wonderful marriage and beautiful children.

One night, we met a man in his forties who had lived a very worldly life in Jordan. Don said that he smoked four to five packs of cigarettes a day and drank hard liquor in large quantities. As a songwriter and a nightclub singer, he had developed a self-serving lifestyle that robbed him of his health and wrecked his marriage. He wanted to kill himself and almost did. Until Jamal reached him. After sensitively sharing Jesus with this nonreligious Muslim, Jamal knew he was ready. When confronted with his sinful problems and the need for forgiveness, Don fell on the floor and began to weep. He stayed there for an hour and a half. He embraced Jesus and was set free from sin and death.

Don now shares Christ effectively and daily. He is also writing Jordanian praise songs. He recently recorded his first CD. He sings and plays the biblical lute instrument. Gone is the depression that once darkened his soul. He has a continual smile. He laughs constantly. Jamal is discipling Don.

★ ✪ ★ ✪

And what you have heard from me in the presence of many witnesses, commit to faithful men who will be able to teach others also. Share in suffering as a good soldier of Christ Jesus.
2 TIMOTHY 2:2–3

Chapter 6

The Believer—
The American

*The complex struggle between religion and politics is
divisive even among American Christians. In Jesus' family,
lines are drawn, and unfair labels are often attached.
Can a believer be pro-Israel, pro-Palestine, and in
favor of the war on terrorism all at the same time?*

Check the Label

Labels are dangerous. Labels are the ultimate way to dismiss someone I don't agree with. If I oppose your view on, let's say, theology, then by labeling you, I reduce you to irrelevance. "Oh, he's just a fundamentalist." "She's a little charismatic, you know." "That church is legalistic." We've all heard them. I confess I have used labels. Lots of them. So did the people around Jesus, and He always put them in their place for stooping to that level. Whether it was egotistical Pharisees or wayward disciples, labeling was out. Jesus wouldn't stand for it. The Savior of the world often spent time with questionable people. To the religious elite, His people-judging skills were suspect for certain. Look at a few of the people Jesus considered important:

- a blind beggar
- a leper
- a Samaritan woman
- an adulterous woman
- a demonized maniac
- a tax extortionist

- a Roman occupying soldier
- a demonized girl from Tyre, the "sin city" of the day

In all of his dealings with people, Jesus never "labeled" them. Each person was valued. Jesus went out of His way to reach those who already had been labeled.

When it comes to Israel and the Middle East, people quickly choose sides and start throwing around labels. I'm talking about Christians here! The intensity of the conflict causes people to formulate opinions regardless of whether they have ever been to the region. It seems so easy—"Can't we all just get along?" The answer of course is a resounding no!

First, it would appear on the surface that born-again Christians are heavily weighted toward Israel's side. Perhaps many Christians see Jerry Falwell, Pat Robertson, and Jack Hayford as high-profile American Christian leaders and assume that their stance is reflective of the majority. Although many pro-Israel American leaders, like the above, are well known and have national platforms, Christianity appears to be fairly split. What is it that determines a person's stance? To answer this, we must examine some of the labels that are, as usual, unfair in nature.

- *Pro-Israel*—Conservative Bible-believing Christians often are thrown into this catchall category. If they interpret prophecy as largely unfulfilled using a literal hermeneutic (interpretation), then they will be immediately placed in this category.
- *Pro-Palestinian*—Christians who do not see the regathering of Israel as a fulfillment of prophecy or react strongly to the enormous humanitarian needs of the Palestinian people often are tagged and put here.

Exposure often is the ultimate deciding factor. On my first visit to Israel, I had a rude awakening to this fact. While staying in Jerusalem with my church's first tour group, I met some West Bank missionaries. They updated us on the challenging ministry in the Palestinian city of Ramallah. The people lived eight miles from Jerusalem, but it was worlds away in living conditions. The Palestinian believers were crushed between rival radical Muslim groups, yet the church was experiencing growth and blessing.

As the conversation turned toward the conflict with Israel, it was easy to detect a bias against the Jews. I expected some of this but was shocked to hear how far the missionaries went. They actually liked Yasser Arafat and thought he was good for the Palestinian people. How could they have an ounce of respect for the Palestinian Authority chairman? I thought he was the top terrorist of all time when considering his malicious accomplishments of the last three decades.

Likewise, I have met missionaries and other leaders who sincerely believe that Israel can do no wrong. This is amazing in light of the fact that Israel's leadership is by the majority secular with strong anti-Christian leanings.

Keep Both Eyes Open

Our primary objective as followers of Jesus Christ is to reach the lost for Him from all nations. Our hope is the salvation plan available for all people, whether Jew or Arab. When going to Israel or ministering there, keeping both eyes open is essential. Jews need Jesus. Arabs need Jesus. This is obvious. The two people groups are completely different in worldview, outlook on life, and goals, yet the bottom line is they are sinners in need of the Lamb of God's sacrifice. There is no question that Israel is God's chosen people. The plan of God has not been ditched in order to "ace" Israel out of a meaningful future. The Abrahamic covenant still has future remaining dividends for Israel. When it comes to salvation, God's love is for all people. This must be at the core of our passion for Israel and the Middle East.

Jewish Roots—Compassionate Heart

I love my Jewish roots! No, I was not born into a Jewish family, but my spiritual roots are thoroughly Jewish. All Christians have Hebraic spiritual roots. Paul said that we are "wild olive shoots" grafted into Israel, the "natural branches." We are to respect them and honor them.

In Romans 11:11–21, Paul laid it out for us:

I ask, then, have they stumbled so as to fall? Absolutely not! On the contrary, by their stumbling, salvation has come to the Gentiles to make Israel jealous. Now if their stumbling brings riches for the world, and their failure riches for the Gentiles, how much more will their full number bring! Now I am speaking to you Gentiles. In view of the fact that I am an apostle to the Gentiles, I magnify my ministry, if I can somehow make my own people jealous and save some of them. For if their being rejected is world reconciliation, what will their acceptance mean but life from the dead? Now if the firstfruits offered up are holy, so is the whole batch. And if the root is holy, so are the branches. Now if some of the branches were broken off, and you, though a wild olive branch, were grafted in among them, and have come to share in the rich root of the cultivated olive tree, do not brag that you are better than those branches. But if you do brag—you do not sustain the root, but the root sustains you. Then you will say, "Branches were broken off so that I might be grafted in." True enough; they were broken off by unbelief, but you stand by faith. Do not be arrogant, but be afraid. For if God did not spare the natural branches, He will not spare you either.

In Scripture, God's emotions are often spent over the children of Israel. God's love for them has known no limits. The prophets also pursued them with the same kind of intensity; so did the apostles. Do I have the same kind of love for Jews? I think that we Christians use Jewish people. We manipulate them. We hustle them like a shady used-car dealer does a first-time buyer. They know it. They have to. After all, Israel is the built-in barometer when it comes to eschatology, the study of future things. We know this since we can compare both Testaments in Scripture and trace their logical end. I confess that I, too, have had a severe case of "end-time fever" at the expense of God's revered covenant people—the Jews.

When I fell in love with Israel, I couldn't get enough of the people. The Bible came alive in a new way for me. Going to the Mount of Olives to see where Jesus ascended from and will return to shows you how real our faith is. Jerusalem is the place that the armies of the world will descend upon in a final attempt to eradicate the "Zionist entity" forever. Revelation 19 and Zechariah 14 record that the nations of the world commit the fatal mistake of underestimating their opponent. The rider on the white horse is none other than the King of Kings and the Lord of Lords. Big mistake. While standing on the Mount of Olives, your mind's eye can see it unfold before you. One day it will happen and then eternity.

How can we as Christians not get caught up in all this cool stuff? The amazing centuries-old predictions continue to come into sharper focus all within our lifetime. The Temple Institute in the old city of Jerusalem is filled with articles that its sponsors plan to use in the coming third temple. The Temple Mount Faithful are considered by the Israeli government as a fringe wacko group. They are committed to building a temple for Yahweh on Mount Moriah some time in the future. It seems hard to believe that a temple could ever be erected in Jerusalem without catapulting all of Islam into World War III. But the group continues with its enthusiasm unabated. They host tour groups that marvel at the exact replicas of the utensils used within Solomon's temple. The candle stands, the high priests' clothes, the incense holders, and the bronze lavers have been redone with the highest attention to detail. Each year the Temple Mount Faithful attempt to bring the uncut cornerstone on an oxcart through the Dung Gate of the old city and place it on the temple platform. There is only one problem that occurs annually with the parade—the Muslims strongly object. So explosive is the event that the Israeli government tries to shut it down before it reaches the gate and sets off another round of rioting. The Muslims wait for the Temple Mount Faithful and unload on them with rocks if they make it through Israeli security.

How will a temple ever be built again? We know from Scripture that the Antichrist will call a halt to temple sacrifice and order all fire offerings to be made to him. Daniel tells us about this future abomination that takes place in the coming next house of God. The temple will be built one way or another. A plausible theory is that an outside group will do the construction, perhaps bypassing an Arab-Israeli showdown in Jerusalem. (I love this stuff! I "overdose" on it. Did you know that the priests, who have to be descendants of the biblical Kohathites, have already been selected? Two hundred of them, in fact. The Jewish name Cohen is the modern family name for the Old Testament Kohathite priesthood.)

What about the centerpiece of the temple itself? What about the ark of the covenant? The very meeting place of God and the high priest? After Israel was safely out of Egypt and Pharaoh's army had become the first sunken navy, God met with Moses to establish this visible point of contact. God would reside over the ark of the covenant, and the coming high priests of Israel would meet Him there face-to-face once every twelve months with fear and trepidation. God's man for the year would enter the Holy of Holies on the Day of Atonement and stand before the presence. "I will meet with you there above the mercy seat, between the two cherubim that are over the ark of the testimony; I will speak with you from there about all that I command you regarding the Israelites" (Exod. 25:22). This was the holy place and the true inner sanctum of Israel's existence for nine hundred years, and then the ark of the covenant vanished.

Where did it go? In his book *In Search of Temple Treasures*, Randall Price quotes Richard Elliot Friedman on the mysterious missing centerpiece: "There is no report that the Ark was carried away, or destroyed, or hidden. There is not even any comment such as, 'And then the Ark disappeared, and we do not know what happened to it' or 'And no one knows where it is to this day.' The most important object in the world, in the Biblical view, simply ceases to be in the story!"[1] Of course, there are a variety of theories about what happened to the ark. Here are four views:

1. Destroyed in Babylonian captivity after being transported to the evil city.
2. Transported to Ethiopia after the supposed affair between King Solomon and the Queen of Sheba.
3. Hidden in the Dead Sea cave region. In the 1990s, expeditions were led there by Vendyl Jones, a former Texas pastor, who is the basis for the character of Steven Spielberg's *Indiana Jones*.
4. Under the Temple Mount. After the Six-Day War of 1967, Israel had control of the Temple Mount. Two rabbis claimed to have found the ark of the covenant in a tunnel under the present-day Dome of the Rock. Israel cemented the entrance to the tunnel, fearing a major Muslim attack.

There are other theories, and nearly every year a new treasure hunter claims to be closing in on finding the elusive ark of the covenant. All of this is fascinating. Third-temple enthusiasts claim that when they are "given the OK" they can have a new temple standing in about nine months. The temple instruments are prepared for usage. From reading our Bibles, we know where all of this is heading. The Antichrist is coming. A temple will be built. The final conflict is in the wings waiting to be played out.

When we examine the news and compare it with Scripture, we see the chess pieces moving into place. Brothers and sisters in Christ, this ought to motivate us into an accelerated all-out service for Jesus. Unfortunately, it usually doesn't. For some reason, prophecy often has a paralytic effect on us. It did on me. Oh yes, I could watch the news and quickly establish a "hot link" to Scripture. Yet I was completely unmoved with compassion for Jews. I was not overwhelmed with pity concerning their coming judgment. I did not seek out Jews with whom to share the Messiah. I did not pray for them. I did not change my lifestyle whatsoever as a result of my keen biblical insight. I say this to my shame.

Maybe you are somewhat like I was. But I have changed. I have been renewed to an active faith. I will no longer sit by and just let it all happen. I will not be a Christian who uses the Jews. Of course, we don't say it, but it is easy to think, *The Jews are back in the land. Israel is a nation again. Jesus is coming back soon.* All of these are, I believe, true statements; yet do our hearts not break for the awful road ahead for Jews themselves? We must have passion for God's people. We must desire the best for them. We must have our hearts broken for these people who face a coming onslaught that will pale by comparison to anything they have ever experienced in their history. Rachel has wept and will weep even more.

What's Best for Israel?

First, every Christian should pray for Israel on an ongoing basis. God commands us to, and there should be no question as to the urgency and necessity of our continual intercession for Israel.

"Pray for the peace of Jerusalem: 'May those who love you prosper; may there be peace within your walls, prosperity within your fortresses'" (Ps. 122:6–7). I won't go into this in depth here. I will cover this in greater detail in chapter 9.

What can America do for Israel? I believe we need to quit forcing Israel into peace treaties that are destined to fail. Israel has had a "go-it-alone" mentality to survive its wars and crucible existence since 1948. Since we in America have been the Israelis' only true friend for decades, we certainly have Israel's ear. I realize that I will be treading on some difficult terrain as I answer my own question here. I love President Bush. I believe he has done a terrific job through one of the most difficult periods in American history. He is God's man for the job, and I do not question this. I am very proud to call George Bush our president. Our historic efforts in Afghanistan and in Iraq have made the world a safer place. When our president declared a war on terrorism, I remember thinking, *Are we in for a long war?* It will be. Make no mistake about it—we are in a twenty-first-century holy war.

That is why many American evangelicals were shocked when President Bush promoted the Road Map for Peace. How could our president call for Israel to give up land that is rightfully hers? After all, should Israel give in to the demands of Palestinian terrorists? Are they any different than the band of thugs we were at war with in Afghanistan or Iraq?

Here's what I believe was really behind it all. Our president wisely put together the road map knowing full well that the current Palestinian leadership would not be able to fulfill their part of the agreement, which is still basically one assignment: stop terrorism. Christians jumped on our president unfairly. I believe that he is calling the Palestinian authority's bluff. Yasser Arafat has no intention of curbing terrorism. He will prove to the world once and for all that he does not desire peace whatsoever. Hopefully, this will drive Palestinians toward moderation and away from the unreasonable and destructive path that their leadership has led them down for five decades.

As the building rubble was still smoldering in New York City after September 11, Israelis were seen weeping openly for Americans who lost their lives in the attack. The sentiments shown toward us as we were suffering from national shock will always be remembered. A magazine cover from Israel read "America and Israel, Fighting Terrorism Together." It seemed we Americans could finally relate to what it is like to live in Israel—in constant danger of fanatical Muslims attempting to blow us all up. What an existence!

Over time, however, our press appeared to employ a double standard when dealing with our enemies and then Israel's. It seems perfectly all right for us to retaliate against our enemies but not so for Israel. I truly am amazed at how our news perceives all of this. Even the normally conservative Fox News often gets it dead wrong. Some news services have equated Israel's army with Palestinian terrorist organizations. Although Israel's army seeks to root out cold-blooded killers, they are often made out to be the culpable themselves. In other words, the mind-set becomes "they deserve it."

Doing ministry in the Gaza Strip is a real eye-opener. We have seen Hamas, Islamic Jihad, and the Al-Aksa Martyrs Brigade, as they say, "up close and personal." These terrorist organizations have no regard for life whatsoever. Not even their own. Did you know that among the Israeli fatalities in the current intifada 75 percent have been civilians? Women and children are specifically targeted. The most vulnerable are taken out without a second thought.

While I was in Israel during the siege of Ramallah, it was reported over the news worldwide that Israel had massacred more than five hundred people. Of course, there were no news people present to verify this, but this was the story spread from supposed eyewitnesses. As it turned out, about fifty were killed, and the terrorist block of the fanatical West Bank city was eliminated. When the numbers were finally verified, no retractions, of course, were issued from news organizations. I certainly cannot vouch for every Israel Defense Force soldier, but I have met many of them, and I do know that it is not a goal to kill the innocent. Sometimes it does happen accidentally, as we have seen before, but Israel apologizes and shows compassion. Its goal is to target the dangerous while protecting the innocent. There is no comparison between Israeli soldiers and Palestinian terrorist organizations, and shame on our news agencies for assuming this.

OK, here's where I may lose some of you. I believe that the Oslo Accords were a big mistake. President Bill Clinton put pressure on Israel, and the message was clear for them: "Give in or pay for it." It's called "sanctions." They work because they affect the economy. Without a healthy dose of American aid and business partnering, Israel's economy could be devastated quickly. Yitzak Rabin was pressured into the Oslo Accords. Benjamin Netanyahu was pressured into the Wye River Accords. Ariel Sharon is being pressured into the Road Map for Peace. No other country could have this sort of sway over Israel. In short, as my friend and writer David Dolan says, "When America speaks, Israel listens." Do they ever!

Of course I want peace. I love the Palestinians who are stuck in a virtual no-man's land. I feel for them. But we have no right to pressure Israel into giving away more land. Can you imagine what we Americans would have thought if after September 11 the majority of the world's nations had unilaterally called for us to forget about the whole thing and concede to the terrorists' wishes? I don't think so! Why should we make Israel do something this absurd?

Let's allow Israel to handle its own war. It's not ours to decide, and we could pay a big price for tying Israeli hands behind their backs and forcing another land-for-peace fiasco. Perhaps we already have paid a big price. . . .

Is America under a Curse?

The Clinton administration pushed Israel into the Oslo Accords. They ultimately fell apart. For the most part, the agreement was applauded by the world and hailed as a great achievement for an American president. Many thought, *Surely this will deliver a comprehensive peace to the region.* Of course, it did not, and the ill-fated Oslo agreement disintegrated before our eyes. Palestinian terror groups stepped up their hate campaign and have not backed down since then.

Was this a great achievement for America? I believe not. I also believe that the penalty for twisting Israel's arm into giving away yet another chunk of land is directly linked to many of our national tragedies. Look at the past decade. Is there a correlation between the 1993 peace treaty and ten years of bloodshed for us in America? You decide.

Since the 1993 Oslo Accords

Feb. 26, 1993: World Trade Center attacked—
bomb exploded in parking garage;
6 persons killed.

Apr. 19, 1995: Oklahoma City federal building attacked—
bomb exploded outside the Alfred P. Murrah
Building; 168 killed.

Nov. 13, 1995: U.S. military camp attacked—
5 killed in Riyadh, Saudi Arabia.

June 25, 1996 U.S. military installation attacked—
in Dhabran, Saudi Arabia, 19 American
soldiers killed.

July 17, 1996   TWA flight 800 crashed after leaving
New York City—several witnesses reported
seeing a surface-to-air missile hit the
aircraft; 230 died.

Aug. 7, 1998   Two American embassies simultaneously
attacked in Kenya and Tanzania (both in
Africa); 224 killed.

Sept. 11, 2001   America attacked in New York City and
Washington, D.C.—World Trade Center
death toll: 2,795; Pentagon death toll: 125;
hijacked flight 93 death toll: 64

With the exception of Oklahoma City bombings and TWA flight 800, all of these attacks against the United States of America are from the very groups we are pressuring Israel to forgive, forget, and give land to. The Oklahoma City bombing, though not carried out by Muslim extremists, has their footprints all over the heinous crime. Timothy McVeigh did meet with Muslim terrorists possibly the day of the attack, according to Joseph Farah, who, in an early 2002 *World Net Daily* article, delineated the alliance that Muslim terrorists and Neo-Nazi groups formed in the early 1990s. The TWA flight 800 probe has been accused of covering up information that suggested a surface-to-air missile shot by a terrorist brought the plane down. We are in the midst of a long, sustained attack on America by Islamic groups that hate us. Not until September 11, 2001, did America realize the problems we face from inside our own country. Our borders have been easy to cross. Undesirables have had almost unlimited access to our nation all in the name of freedom.

I was able to see this firsthand myself in August of 2002 on a flight back from the Middle East. Our flight schedule was from Abu Dhabi, United Arab Emirates, to Amman, Jordan, on to Frankfort, Germany, then to Chicago, and finally to Denver. The flying marathon takes a toll. While on the third leg of the flight just after takeoff from Germany, I was hoping to get some badly needed sleep. I noticed that the flight attendant crew was huddled in the middle of the 747 and obviously disturbed about something. The attendants looked nervous and very concerned. I got out of my seat and asked if everything was OK. They assured me that it was and to please return to my seat. I tried to probe a little further, so I put the question this way: "Look, I work in the Middle East, and my dad is also an FBI agent. You people look very scared. Are you worried about a passenger on this plane?"

They immediately opened up. There was a passenger in 29G who looked Middle Eastern, and he was staring at the flight attendants with anger on his face. He also was opening up all the compartments in the bathroom as if he was trying to hide something. One of the young ladies remarked that because the cockpit was locked for the flight, the attendants were on their own. No wonder they were panicking. A call was placed to the pilots who in turn called the FAA to check on the suspicious passenger. The FAA notified the FBI to do a quick background check, and they found out the news everyone dreaded. He was from Iraq and single. Not good! Somehow he had made it through security and was on his way to the United States. So much for my nap.

The plot started to thicken. A man in first class started to look back at the man in 29G and make eye contact with him continually. He looked to be communicating with him. Now the passengers in first class started to get nervous. The man was also Middle Eastern and was not only rude to everyone around him but appeared hostile. Another background check uncovered another single man from Iraq. This was not looking good. The flight was a long one, and nothing ended up happening other than the two Iraqis exchanging looks and nods. When we landed, we noticed the two men walk right through passport control and security with ease. *What in the world is going on?* we thought. Later, we saw the relieved flight attendants, and they told us that the FBI was tailing the two Iraqis to see where they were going and whom they were seeing. So the plan was to let them through and see if they could find some bigger fish from the terrorist underworld. We live in a dangerous time as Americans.

Could it be a judgment of God on us for our involvement in the ill-fated Oslo agreement? After all, who are we to give away God's land anyway? I guess if I didn't believe this, I would be guilty of a very proud heart. If I didn't believe this, I would be thinking that we in America received some sort of special exemption from the Abrahamic covenant. God is faithful and consistent in His dealings with mankind. How can we curse Israel and reap no fallout? Nobody else has throughout history. I can't help believing that the ice we're currently walking on is getting awfully thin!

What's the Answer?

We just support Israel and let the Israelis handle their own security issues. They certainly don't tell us what to do or sanction us. They've shown they are completely capable in the past. It is as simple as that. America is right to fight the war on terrorism for as long as it takes. When it comes to Israel, let them work out their terrorist problems, and we'll work on ours because the solution that is always proposed to Israel is for them to give up more land.

Any plan that calls for Israel to give up land for peace will fail. Like his predecessors, Ariel Sharon is not for it but will sign it because of American pressure. The Israelis are not stupid. They know what it means if they hold out. Possible U.S. sanctions were being discussed with them as I wrote this: "The State Department confirmed . . . that Israel's continued construction of a controversial West Bank security barrier may result in U.S. financial sanctions."[2] If Israel refuses to sign, a few things might happen:

- Israel might no longer be able to use American military hardware in its conflict against terrorism. Recently, I watched an Apache helicopter fire at a Muslim bomb-making factory. This would be illegal if the road map is adopted.
- Israel might be severely penalized economically if it refuses to accept the peace plan. Israeli businessmen know this and have begun to put their own pressure on Prime Minister Sharon.

We should not treat Israel this way; they don't deserve it. The future health of our nation is at stake. Will we bless them or curse them?

What's Best for Palestinians?

I'm sure at this point some readers think that I don't have a heart for Palestinians. That couldn't be farther from the truth. Their situation is so difficult that while visiting wonderful Palestinian believers I am in anguish. Yes, I believe that this is Israel's land—all of it—but that doesn't mean that I don't care for the Palestinians. I do. They have been manipulated and used for decades. Their own leadership has abused them for unattainable religious goals to prove Islam is the superpower of the world. It has failed on all fronts. The Palestinian people who suffer needlessly are no better off now than they were in 1948. Their leadership has failed, wouldn't you agree?

Let's Start Over

In the twentieth century, the physical landscape of the world changed dramatically. As the Turkish Ottoman Empire collapsed in 1917, the area went from being a vast empire spanning an entire region to several smaller national entities. In the West, we merely viewed these changes on our maps as the newly formed nations looked like a big jigsaw puzzle coming together. But millions of people were affected, and their lives changed forever. The massive people shifting became one great big migration perhaps never seen in history. From the former Turkish Ottoman Empire, France and Britain designed new states that included Syria, Lebanon, Iraq, and Jordan. The process began to take shape in the 1920s. The British had thought long and hard about placing Jews within the region. A national home for them had been promised, but as the nations came into existence, the Jews' piece of the pie continued to shrink. The Palestine mandate included present-day Jordan. This would have made Israel comparable to the other nations in size. All of that changed in 1921, when the entire area of Jordan, called Transjordan, was taken out of the equation for the Jews. Eighty percent of the land previously drawn up as a future home for them was gone.

In the Arab world, tribal battles were common before the Middle East countries were established. *Lawrence of Arabia* was the movie that brought Arab tribal wars to the big screen. Although the film was exaggerated to some degree, it depicted the strife rampant throughout the Arabian Peninsula in that time period. One ruler caught up in the conflict was King Abdullah, who was defeated in one of the wars. He was literally a king without a kingdom. In an effort to resolve this, Abdullah was given the Transjordan. His kingdom became the home for his Hashemite tribe. The Hashemites believe they are descendants of Muhammad. The country reflected this as it became off-limits to any Jewish settlements. The country was predominantly filled with Palestinian Arabs rather than Hashemites. Even today Jordan is about 70 percent Palestinian.

When the partition plan went to the United Nations for a vote, the proposed land size for Israel was one-tenth of what had been originally promised to them. The desperate, homeless Jews took what they were given, but it was a great injustice.

Israel's future was sifted through a complex political system. In 1948, more land was taken from them. Arabs were also given biblical Judea and Samaria, and Jordan incorrectly named it the West Bank. The Gaza Strip also was given to Arabs. The land is actually Israel's and should be called the "East Bank" to be geographically correct. The very fact that the territory was named the West Bank uncovers Jordan's intent to seize the land from the beginning. What remained for Jews were three strips of land. The land was not even connected. As for Jerusalem, Jews were merely given access to their most prized possession. Israel was clearly cheated in the whole process.

To make matters even worse, Jordan incorporated the West Bank in 1950. Egypt took the Gaza Strip. When the two territories were run by Jordan and Egypt, respectively, they were never called "occupied." There was also no talk of a Palestinian state at that time. When this land was taken from Israel, there was not a flicker of interest within the Arab world. When Israel won back the land in the Six-Day War of 1967, the outcries began.

What about Refugees?

Now that all of that is said about Israel receiving such an unfair deal, what about refugees? I must confess I was very unsympathetic to the needs of the Palestinians until I visited their refugee camps. Regardless of how they got there, the conditions are some of the worst anywhere. In our ministry at EvangeCube, we try to help the Palestinians in the camps with food distribution and have plans to have a mission trip of young people to repair the shanties barely standing. I asked myself several questions as the shock of their five decades of history sunk in.

- How would I like to live this way?
- Would I be able to fight off the bitterness that so many of them exhibit?

- How would I get my family out of there for good?
- What would it be like to live in a tent for fifty years?

In February 2003, the *Jerusalem Post* published an excellent section within the paper titled "Refugees Forever?" It began this way: "Unique about the Palestinian refugee problem is that it has been allowed—even forced—to continue and to grow. Every other major refugee group has been resettled within a generation. Of the approximately 135 million refugees created over the last century, only the Palestinians have retained this dismal, nationless status."[3]

Estimated Figures

- 1.25 million Greeks and 500,000 Turkish refugees resettled
- 13 million Germans ejected from their ancestral homeland in East Prussia, Silesia, and the Sudentenland by the Advancing Russian forces in World War II, resettled
- 440,000 Finns reabsorbed
- 9 million Hindus and Sikhs left Pakistan for India and 6.5 million Muslims fled India for Pakistan
- 9 million Koreans fled Communist rule to South Korea
- 4.5 million Poles resettled
- 2 million Jews fled Europe and Arab states
- 900,000 Vietnamese took to the sea in order to avoid Communist rule
- 700,000 Chinese fled to Hong Kong
- 2,000,000 Hutus and Tutsis fled ethnic massacres in Rwanda for Zaire
- Untold masses were forced from their homes in ethnically torn former Yugoslavia
- 2 million Afghans fled Taliban rule en masse, most taking shelter in Pakistan

Refugees Created by Conflicts
- 1917–1933:   8,500,000
- 1933–1945:   73,200,000
- 1945–1957:   53,650,000

The Sad Paradox

In 1947, while Britain was disengaging from Palestine, it was also withdrawing from India, leading to the birth of independent Pakistani and Indian states. Whereas the Arab-Israeli conflict created hundreds of thousands of refugees, the Indians and Pakistanis wisely agreed to transfer millions of their people across the border in order to diffuse ethnic and religious tensions. India sent Muslims to Pakistan, which in turn sent Hindus to India. Both states granted citizenship to these refugees. The much smaller—and perhaps even more solvable— problem of Arab refugees is a sad paradox, in that it has cost the Western world so many billions of dollars in humanitarian aid that only perpetuates the refugees' plight, and has monopolized its media attention for over half a century, when alternatives in refugee transfers such as the one between India and Pakistan have proven effective.

Excerpted from The Arabs in History *(Oxford University Press) by Prof. Bernard Lewis, leading expert on Islamic and Middle Eastern history.*

That's what makes the situation so difficult. I minister among Palestinians and consider them some of my closest friends. Their situation is miserable. These believers conduct meaningful, life-transforming ministry in the lives of countless people. They are vital. Many of the Muslims I have met in Palestinian areas are far from what I would expect them to be. Yes, Gaza is home to some of the world's most dangerous terrorist groups. It is also home to many kind-hearted Arab families. Their culture is one of the most beautiful anywhere. If you knock on an Arab door, they will invite you into their house no matter who you are. They have to; it's a core virtue for them to be hospitable to all people.

Here is the problem. The Palestinian people are being duped by their leaders. Their leaders cannot come up with an agenda that doesn't have outrageous Islamic goals. Only God can pull Arab culture out of the smothering grasp of Islam. For thirteen centuries it has shaped Arab culture that was fragmented into tribes. Islam has successfully kept the Palestinians from moving one inch forward by turning hatred for Israel into the main issue. Privately many Palestinians, whether Christian or Muslim, are frightened about what the future holds in a Palestinian state. They would not discuss this openly or they would be considered traitors or Jew-lovers.

The corruption of the Palestinian Authority is legendary. Billions of dollars have gone straight into Yasser Arafat's bank accounts and have done nothing to help feed and clothe the Palestinians. Recently, the chairman's personal wealth was estimated to be $3.1 billion. This was detailed in the August 2002 edition of ArabicNews.com. Israeli intelligence sources revealed this staggering total, and it was unchallenged by the Palestinian Authority. How tragic this is in light of the fact that the average Palestinian lives on a little less than two dollars a day. They are the ultimate pawns in the chess game Islam continues to play with Israel. There is no reason that homes couldn't have been built with all the money that has vanished from the people and gone straight to the Palestinian Authority.

A startling example of the vast corruption was uncovered a few years ago when a Palestinian broke into Arafat's compound and was able to prove where billions of dollars had been stashed. In the December 5, 1999, *London Telegraph*, Palestinians discussed their break-in of Arafat's office in Tunis. Not only was there an enormous amount of money in the chairman's foreign bank accounts, but they discovered that he owned stock too. Arafat and the PA, it seems, own shares on the Frankfurt, Paris, and Tokyo stock exchanges. The chairman also owns stock in the German car giant Mercedes Benz. This man has bucks! He is loaded with stolen funds taken for decades from the people. No wonder Saddam Hussein sent suicide bomber reward money directly to the parents' home. If it went through Palestinian Authority offices, it wouldn't have made it to the people.

Israel will always be the ultimate bull's-eye on the Islamic dartboard. Israel will be blamed for every problem the Palestinians experience. It is the only explanation that Islam can come up with. In counseling, I remember saying many times, "The only person you cannot help is the one who doesn't have a problem." The refusal to see this perpetuates the cycle of Palestinian misery. But could we possibly expect Palestinians to stand up and overthrow their leadership? They are controlled and without any resources to do such a thing. Refugees need so much in the way of basic necessities. The needs are enormous, and I believe we can help.

What an obvious contrast there is between light and darkness as seen in people's lives. I want Palestinians to have a better life. *I want them to enjoy freedom and to have their children educated to ensure a good future! I want the best for them.*

Here are two Palestinian reforms that are badly needed:

1. Give the Palestinian Authority a major overhaul. How sad it is to see the dismal living conditions that the Palestinians endure year after year compared to the Israeli standard of living. Arab Israelis and Jewish Israelis enjoy their health care system, the right to vote, and government assistance that they receive for each child in their family. Palestinians would flourish in a system like that! Yet, they will never have these things in a Palestinian State. A dictator will run it unless the people demand something better. Many Palestinians

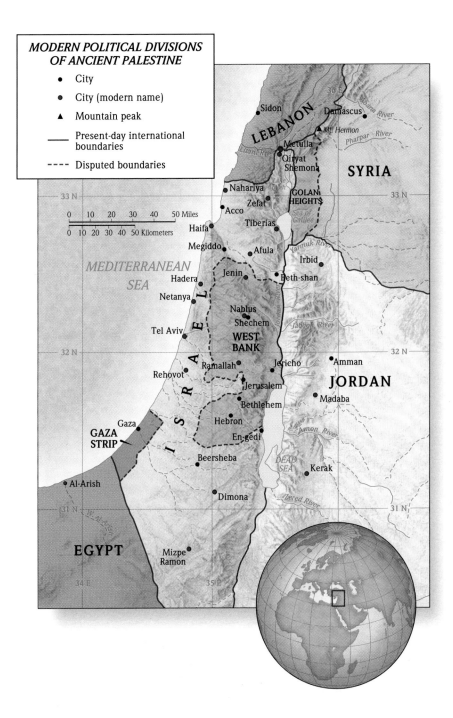

MODERN POLITICAL DIVISIONS
OF ANCIENT PALESTINE

● City

● City (modern name)

▲ Mountain peak

—— Present-day international
boundaries

---- Disputed boundaries

Jerusalem—CITY OF RELIGIOUS PASSION

Rabbi at the Western Wall

Young Orthodox at the wall

Orthodox Jews on Mount of Olives

Jewish prayer warrior

Warriors of another kind

Wounded Israeli soldier and his fiancee

Israeli soldiers on break at McDonalds

Jewish children at play in a narrow street of Old City ❯

Two generations of Jerusalem

Traditional
Jews in
Jerusalem

**Jerusalem—
The Old Holy City**

". . . and My people who are called by My name humble themselves,
pray and seek My face, and turn from their evil ways, then I will hear
from heaven, forgive their sin, and heal their land."   2 Chronicles 7:14

*Tel Aviv—
The New Secular City*

Gaza—FRONTLINE SCENERY

Arafat's call to take Jerusalem

Arafat's bombed head-quarters. Notice the mosque untouched

لا ... ولن يكتمل حلمي
الابك ياقدس

Israel to Gaza welcome

"SAFE PASSAGE"
TO GAZA STRIP

Gaza grafitti honoring killed youth and Hamas

Traditional Gaza taxi

Young and Old in the

REFUGEES

From sweet sisters and a four-year-old boy. . .

Gaza Refugee Camps

. . . *to a one-hundred-year-old woman and entire families, they are*

REFUGEES

Gaza refugee children

Gaza Muslims with author   *Gaza Awana Club*

TAKING THE GOSPEL TO THE PEOPLE OF THE MIDDLE EAST

"For everyone who calls on the name of the Lord will be saved." Romans 10:13

JoAnn Doyle with Egyptian baby

Nazareth child

Gaza Muslims

Bethlehem priest

Palestinian woman praying for her children

Jordan—THE HASHEMITE KINGDOM

Traditional Jordanian dress

Jordan's kings *Jordanian youth*

JORDANIAN EVANGECUBE TRAINING

Arab believers of all ages

Iraq

In Saddam's throne room, picture of missiles pointed at Israel

Ambassador to Iraq Paul Bremer, left, and author Tom Doyle

Iraqi youth

Iraqi family

Iraqi believers

Traditional Islamic dress

Young Saddam supporter arriving with Lisa Lalani from EvangeCube

Watchman on the Wall

31 Days of Prayer for the People of Israel

DAY	PLACE
1	Jerusalem
2	East Jerusalem
3	Tel Aviv
4	Nablus
5	Haifa
6	Jenin
7	Tiberias
8	Ramallah
9	Nazareth
10	Jericho
11	Jaffa
12	Bethlehem
13	Ashkelon
14	Hebron
15	Beersheba
16	The Gaza Strip
17	Caesarea
18	Tulkarm
19	Netanya
20	Palestinian Refugee Camps
21	Eilat
22	Latrun
23	Hadera
24	Jewish Kibbutzim
25	Safed
26	Acco
27	Kiryat Shmona
28	Afula
29	Ashdod
30	Israeli Government Offices
31	PA Leadership

27.Kiryat Shmona
25.Safed
Sea of Galilee
7.Tiberias
26.Acco
9.Nazareth
5.Haifa
28.Afula
6.Jenin
17.Caesarea
23.Hadera
19.Netanya
S A M A R I A
Mediterranean
18.Tulkarm
Sea
4.Nablus
3.Tel Aviv
11.Jaffa
8.Ramallah
10.Jericho
22.Latrun
2.East Jerusalem
29.Ashdod
1.Jerusalem
12.Bethlehem
13.Ashkelon
14.Hebron
J U D E A
16.The Gaza Strip
Dead Sea
15.Beersheba
I S R A E L
21.Eilat

Here's What to Pray

...for Gospel exposure and conversions.
...for churches to grow and plant new churches.
...for Biblical reconciliation between Jews and Arabs.
...for revival to spread to the rest of the Middle East.
...for all mission groups in the area:
   EvangeCube
   Global Missions Fellowship
   The International Mission Board
   Campus Crusade
   Youth with a Mission (to name a few)

Map by Jennifer Shipley

live in tents and shacks, while their leaders live in lavish mansions off of the foreign aid that was supposed to improve living conditions for the people. Unless the people rise up and say "no more," Islamic extremism will continue to be the machine that runs their culture, and the Palestinians will pay dearly for it. Today in the Gaza Strip, the Hamas terrorist group is in charge of all medical care. That ought to give us a picture of what lies ahead for the Palestinians.

Palestinian Christians will have a rude awakening if the Palestinian State becomes a reality. I believe religious freedom will become nonexistent. This is vastly different then what Palestinians have experienced with Israel's government. The Israelis have destroyed no mosques since 1948. Not one. In wars and in all conflicts, they go out of their way to protect Islamic places of prayer and worship. My eyes were opened to this fact on my first visit to the Gaza Strip. The Israelis had bombed Chairman Arafat's compound after the P. A. had launched several suicide attacks. The compound was a mess. It looked like a tornado scene in Kansas. The buildings were flattened and destroyed. There was no one killed in the bombings as the chairman was in Ramallah at the time. One building stood in perfect shape among the rubble. It was Arafat's personal mosque. The golden dome on it is a mini version of Jerusalem's Dome of the Rock. It was not even nicked. Even in the midst of the intifada that had cost Israel hundreds of innocent lives, Muslim religious buildings were still respected. Israel used pinpoint bombing techniques to ensure that.

What frightens so many Palestinian believers is what they will face when they are under a government that has absolutely no regard for religious freedom.

Palestinian terrorists have destroyed or desecrated hundreds of Jewish synagogues over their fifty-six years of coexistence with Israelis. One of the holiest places in all of Israel is found in the biblical city of Shechem, where Joseph the patriarch is buried. In October of 2000, when Prime Minister Ehud Barak pulled the military out of the West Bank as a concession mandated by the Oslo Accords, the trouble began almost immediately at the tomb. Within hours of Israel's departure from the holy place, Joseph's tomb was set on fire and the dome was painted green and declared an Islamic mosque. This was never denounced by the Palestinian Authority and remains a mosque to this day. Imagine what awaits Palestinian Christians if they dare take issue with their leadership under a Palestinian State. Religious freedom is not on the radar screen of the Palestinian Authority, whether it be for Jews or Christians.

The time is now for moderate Palestinian Muslims and Christians to overhaul the P. A. and its corrupt leadership that will control their lives with an iron fist once in power. It's still not too late. Privately, Palestinians talk about the scores of people who are fed up and ready to pay the price for a "regime change." I pray that they follow through.

2. Start over—minus the terrorist groups. So much would change if the unrealistic radical Islamic goals were dropped for the good of the Palestinian people. In short, the Palestinians want a place to live, but their leadership has tweaked this and turned it all into a campaign to eradicate Israel. If terrorist groups were booted out of Palestinian areas and if the Palestinian Authority came up with reasonable goals, much could be achieved. Here are a few givens:

- Israel isn't going away. Why should the Palestinians waste their effort in trying to accomplish the impossible? It's only a twisted dream.
- Palestinians need viable representation. Most of them do not have a latent loathing of Jews. Many Palestinians have worked with Jews before. Many have benefited personally from them. It has been done.
- Face the truth. Islam's outrageous goals are put ahead of human needs. Palestinians need to do a "root canal" on their leadership and drive out fanatical Muslim extremists. If not, they could stay in tents forever. It's time to wake up and smell the hummus!
- Israel is willing to share the land. It has proven this over and over for decades.

To some, my conclusions will offend. Palestinians become Israeli Arabs? Right! Many have and live the life they always dreamed. But I say this with all seriousness. A democratic Jewish-led government will beat an Islamic dictatorship any day of the week. My heart breaks for the Palestinian people each time I enter the West Bank or the Gaza Strip.

Something must be done, and something can. If they absorb into Israel and drop the Islamically driven refugee project, they will realize their dream finally. If not Israeli Arabs, why not erase the blackboard and begin afresh with new leadership that will put the people first and put aside unattainable goals derived from irrational fundamental Islam?

Love a Palestinian—Give 'Em Jesus

Jesus is the answer. In Palestinian areas it's no different. My desire is to see every Palestinian in Israel and throughout the Middle East hear a clear presentation of the gospel. They are responding when given Jesus in a loving, nonconfrontational manner.

Palestinians often feel that because America often sides with Israel the implication is that Palestinians are hated. But this I believe is an unfair charge. I do believe that the bulk of Christian ministry efforts have benefited Jewish believers at the expense of Palestinian believers. It is quite noticeable just how few ministries work with the Palestinians. This is a sad fact.

But as an American I can be pro-Israel, which means that I believe the Jews have a biblical right to the land that God gave them and a political right to the land that the United Nations gave them. I can be pro-Palestinian, which means that I believe Palestinians can benefit greatly from a shared existence with Israel. As much as I want Israelis to be protected and preserved, I want Palestinians to be prosperous and provided for. That's why I am strongly behind our president's initiative that declared war on terrorism. This part is essential. As Palestinians extract this element from their society, they will see light at the end of the tunnel. Pro-Israel, pro-Palestinian. The answer is Jesus. Cynical Jewish agnostics have been delivered into His awaiting arms of grace. Angry Palestinians have escaped swimming in a sea of bitterness and now are celebrating in living water instead. Christians, please don't ever sit at home, watch the news, and think the whole mess can be solved politically. If it was that way, it would have been ironed out decades ago.

As American believers, we cannot continue to show a widespread lack of concern for the suffering Palestinian population. Biblical solutions are available. Through compassionate acts, we can meet their needs and still honor Israel. We believe Israel is to be supported, and that this pleases the heart of God. We also should believe that we must act like the followers of Jesus no matter how the Palestinian quagmire developed. Jesus honored Israel and still loved some of their enemies at the same time. Why can't we?

The Vise Grip Tightens—the Revival Begins

Jews are reachable. Palestinians are reachable. The church is the strongest and healthiest when it is persecuted. The worst places to be a believer in the world are really the best places to see the church in action. Our spiritual vitality blooms in treacherous places. The *Voice of the Martyrs* (May 2003 edition) detailed the awful persecution that Palestinians endure if they convert from Islam to Christianity. "When Ali was a young boy, he listened to Palestine Liberation Organization radio broadcasts that target him to hate Christians and Jews. He would often pray in the Mosque and ask Allah to destroy Jews, Americans, and non-Muslims. When Ali first visited a church in 1997, he was shocked to hear the pastor talk about loving one's enemies. The pastor preached about how God loves all people but hates our sins. 'That touched my heart.' In the Islamic faith, there is no love for non-Muslims or our enemies like in Christianity. Ali started to attend church regularly, because for the first time in his life, he felt love, joy, and peace."[4]

Ali was interrogated and beaten and ordered to stop attending church. He was even shown the letter that the Mufti of Jerusalem signed ordering a *fatwa*, which is a call for a death sentence. The article went on: "About three years later, Ali was blindfolded and kidnapped by the Palestinian Security Police. His hands and feet were tied together, and he was hung from the rafters with his feet dangling just above the ground. He was beaten with sticks and electric cables."[5]

Ali was stuck in a solitary confinement cell for three weeks in Nablus. Nablus is a West Bank city that in biblical days was called Shechem. It is also the place where Jacob's favorite son Joseph was buried after his bones were brought back to Israel from Egypt. Nablus has become a bastion for Muslim fundamentalism. The Hamas have a military style training ground there. Brazenly, these radical Muslims burned

Joseph's tomb, which was an important holy site to Jews, and turned it into a mosque.

Ali prayed that God would provide for his family as he was incarcerated. "On April 4, 2002, Israeli tanks entered Nablus in an attempt to crush the intifada and destroy Hamas suicide bomb factories. Ali was freed from his prison cell; as a result Ali was surprised and elated by his freedom. He recalled the words of Jesus to love your neighbor as yourself. Without hesitation, Ali raced toward the advancing Israeli soldiers and kissed the gun turret of one of their tanks. He thanked God for answering his prayer and vowed to remain faithful to Jesus, his true liberator and source of eternal freedom."[6]

This is one of many of Muhammad's followers who has seen the light and left Islam for good. The call of Jesus is strong enough to liberate Muslims from their sins. It is also strong enough to liberate new believers from the fear of death after their conversion. Former Muslims who have professed Christ amaze me. They give up their lives for Jesus. If they avoid being killed by former fellow Muslims, their lives are made miserable for their "high crime." They lose jobs. They lose their family ties, which are strongest in Arab culture. They jeopardize everything dear to them. They suffer. As I said before, Jewish converts will be shunned by their families if they become believers. Muslim converts can expect the same treatment and often worse. In many cases they will be killed, and the family member who performs the dirty deed will believe he is in line to receive a special blessing from Allah when he arrives in paradise one day. Despite the incredible risks, Muslims have never been more open to Jesus Christ as their Savior.

Abigail Lytle was not a typical fourteen-year-old living on the coast of the Mediterranean city of Haifa just below Mount Carmel. Her father distributes the *Jesus* film in the area, and the family has made a conscious effort to live in Israel despite the risks they face. In the spring of 2003, the intifada was escalating, and the father decided to have a family meeting. He talked to his children about the situation and said they probably should begin plans for a move back to America. It was too unsafe, especially in a Jewish community. The children prayed about it for a few days and then came back to their mom and dad with their advice. The five children all agreed that God had them there for a reason. They had been called as a family to reach the lost sheep of Israel, and they believed God would use their lives in a great way if they were obedient to His call.

Young Abigail had become involved in a children's teaching program that brought Jewish and Arabic children together in an effort to encourage successful coexistence. The class was preparing for an upcoming encounter with Arab youth in a few days. Abigail was bright and full of joy and optimism about her future in Israel. She had been raised in Israel because her father came to the land to work in the technological field. He later was on staff at a Baptist church. Abigail loved life and was a creative young lady. Her family remembers her all-out trust in God and her fearlessness despite living in a land continually at war.

On March 5, 2003, Abigail was traveling on a city bus near the Carmel center and moving toward Haifa University. In an instant, a suicide bomber pulled on the trigger and exploded the bus. The bomb devastated the bus as seventeen people were killed and fifty-three were injured. The scene was a usual one in Israel because the murderer had strapped the explosives to his own body and placed metal shrapnel within the device to maximize the number of injuries. Abigail was only a few rows away from the man and was killed instantly. Her parents' worst fears were realized as they arrived at the charred bus: Abigail was gone from them.

What happened afterward was from the realm of the miraculous. Abigail's death attracted widespread attention. Her story of deciding to stay and help Israeli Jews was all over the news since she was an American born in New Hampshire.

The press coverage was magnified and went global. Young Abigail reminded me of Cassie Bernall at Colorado's Columbine High School. Her unshakable faith in the midst of a life-threatening situation was used by God to reach people across the world.

Abigail's funeral was broadcast in Israel on live TV. The Israeli government sent a senior official to attend the service. Her pastor talked about Abigail's life in depth. He also shared that Abigail's confidence in God was because of her loving relationship with Jesus Christ. This was a first in Israel. The gospel was being heard all over the country. It was also being beamed across the world simultaneously. I watched it in Colorado. Abigail's life was unique in that she was not Jewish, yet blended so well into Jewish culture.

In Israel, funerals are often gloomy and despairing. This one was not. Abigail's parents made a conscious effort to express their grief and to lay it all on Jesus. The ceremony was marked by hope and faith in the One who said, "I am the resurrection and the life. The one who believes in Me, even if he dies, will live" (John 11:25).

Senior Knesset member Yuval Stenitz represented the government. He remarked later that he had witnessed more than the power of religion at the service. "He had seen the vigor of faith. A TV reporter, hardened after having been assigned to many a funeral (and Israel has many such these days) confessed that he was deeply moved, even to tears, by what he had seen. A week later, the Haifa municipality was still astir as officials spoke of the amazing funeral. The sense of communal affection was also outstandingly uncommon to the average Israeli mind."[7]

Abigail's life touched more people at once than her family's ministry ever could have in their lifetimes. The next encounter meeting for the Arab Jewish youth was dedicated to Abigail and her friend Yuoal, who also gave her life up that day.

Abigail's father, Phillip, could never have shown the *Jesus* film to that many people in decades of faithful service. Jesus took young Abigail home, and her departure brought Him glory all over the land that He loves. Jesus was exalted and seen in Israel as the real answer to life's deepest problems in this hurting region. The irony of the situation is that Abigail's pastor, named Samuel, is Arab. An Arab preaching at a predominantly Jewish funeral. Only Jesus could orchestrate all of that. Samuel pastors a Jewish congregation. How's that for reconciliation? A non-Jewish American girl gave her life for Jews. An Arab pastor serves Jews. All of it was wrapped up together neatly by God Himself. The result? The majority of Israel was given the privilege of hearing and seeing what Jesus is really about.

Ali, the Ramallah believer, is now free of all of the hatred stewing around him. So are Abigail's parents even though the loss of their precious daughter is devastating. Remarkably, they plan to stay in Israel. Pastor Samuel is also free from the bitterness between Arabs and Jews. Abigail is free and home enjoying the presence of Jesus Himself. In all cases, Satan lost. Jesus won.

As Americans, when we truly want the best for people, we may not fit nicely in a category. Labels won't fit either. I am pro-Israel. I want the best for the Israelis, and that includes keeping the land that is rightfully theirs. I am pro-Arab. I want the best for the Arabs, and that includes overcoming radical Islam, the religion that makes killing the ultimate answer for everything. I am in favor of the war on terrorism; it is a just war.

More important than being an American today is obviously being a believer in Jesus Christ. We possess the key that unlocks the spiritual stronghold chains that are squeezing Israel. In the end, Jesus is the only One who can make a difference. Only He can transform the hearts of those in conflict. Without Him, it will never end.

★ ✪ ★ ✪

Dvat and Eyal—
Modern-Day Ruth and Boaz

THE COUPLE IS STUNNING. In their early twenties, Eyal and Dvat are an Israeli version of Ken and Barbie. The lovers, however, are much more than a couple of sharp-looking Jewish youth. The depth of their life experience rivals those of people twice their age. Their journey took an unexpected turn on August 4, 2002. The devastation that the two of them have had to deal with at such a young age reeks of injustice. They do not complain.

In the summer of 2002, Eyal and Dvat "had life by the tail." Dvat was studying to be a lawyer. She is Jewish, but her family roots are from Iraq. Before 1948, many Jews lived in Baghdad and surrounding Iraqi communities. After Israel became a nation again, most Muslim-led nations forced Jews to leave. The refugee problem for Jews led families to Israel from all Middle East countries. Jews from Africa and Europe also were displaced and arrived steadily. Dvat loves life, and her smile lights up the room. She is focused and well disciplined. She has maintained this even in the midst of the three-year-old war in her homeland.

Eyal is strong and taller than most Israeli young men. He is handsome and well spoken. Since Israeli's population is so small, every young person is required to serve in the military. Men and women both serve unless there are religious objections. The ultra-Orthodox who are so often seen at the Western Wall praying and wearing black hats and side curls, traditionally do not allow their children to enter the military. Men serve an average of two years, and women serve at least six months. The system works because it gives Israelis a vested interest in the country. Antiwar demonstrations are almost nonexistent here.

Eyal was in the midst of fulfilling his obligation to his country. He was moving up in the military, and his options were many because of his fine service within the Israeli Defense Forces (IDF).

Eyal was going to his military assignment on that hot August day. He was traveling on bus number 361 from the coastal city of Haifa to the Galilean city of Safed. Under the direction of the Hamas terrorist group, a suicide bomber detonated his hidden weapon of destruction at the Meron junction. The bus exploded instantly. Nine people were murdered, and fifty were wounded. To many Americans, it was only another lead news story from the turbulent Middle East. In Colorado Springs, I watched it and turned away in disgust.

Months later, while in Tel Aviv, we were introduced to Eyal, who had numerous physical problems. He recounted what it was like to be on that bus. Eyal had been visiting with others on the bus when the killer hopped on board, grabbed a soldier around the waist, and blew himself up in Allah's name. Among terrorists, the more IDF one kills or maims, the better. This bus was loaded with soldiers. Three sergeants were killed in the heinous attack.

Eyal was one meter away when the terrorist pushed the button and exploded the moving vehicle. Immediately, Eyal could not see. He felt enormous pain in one of his legs and pulled something out that had impaled it. Only when he felt a shoe on the end did he realize it was another soldier's leg that had been blown off. The scene, of course, was mass chaos. Rushed to the hospital, the wounded were taken to surrounding area trauma centers. There were too many to handle in one hospital. Some of the dead were twenty feet away, waiting to catch another bus. Eyal was within four feet and lived.

Dvat has supported Eyal through numerous surgeries. He was told that he would never walk again. He walks. He was told that his brain could not function properly and that they should just pull the plug on life support. His long-term and short-term memory has returned. He has hearing aids to amplify sounds.

He needs an eye transplant someday when it becomes available. He is a miracle several times over.

Eyal and Dvat have a true love story. It would have been easier for Dvat to move on and end their relationship. The road ahead is very long. He does not look much like the man that she fell in love with a few years ago. But love won. Through their uphill existence and their daily struggles, God has strengthened their resolve and bonded them together for life. They plan to marry on August 4, 2004, the second anniversary of the bus bombing. This is their way of redeeming the day for good by not letting evil win. They have hope. They smile. They walk confidently toward the future hand in hand. Radical Islam lost on August 4, 2002.

Dvat gives endless attention to her fallen soldier. Like Ruth's of the Old Testament, her steady attitude and loyalty to Eyal are part of a real-life Hebrew romance. They are helplessly in love, committed together for life, and unshakable in their confidence that one day Eyal will be able to see again.

★ ☆ ★ ☆

For wherever you go, I will go, and wherever you live,
I will live; your people will be my people, and your God
will be my God. Where you die, I will die, and there I
will be buried. May the LORD do this to me, and even more,
if anything but death separates you and me.
RUTH 1:16–17

MAXIMIZING THE MOMENT

The American church is at a critical juncture.
God wants to use us to influence the nation of Israel
on its journey back to God. He also wants us to participate
in the Middle East revival that has already begun with
Arabs and Jews. This is the mission heart of God.
We must pray as never before. We must also wake up
the sleeping giant of our day—the Western church.
America has sent the gospel around the world.
Now we need the power of the gospel
to return to our shores.

Chapter 7

The Mission Heart of God

God intends to use the church to bring Israel to its senses and Arab nations to repentance in the future. More Jews and Muslims have converted to Christianity in the past few years than in the last several centuries. It is time to hear the good news from the Middle East.

Mission Central

The greatest enterprise in all of history is the New Testament church. Listen to the greatness of what God is in the midst of accomplishing by His great power through Christ and His beloved church:

> So then, remember that at one time you were
> Gentiles in the flesh—called "the uncircumcised" by
> those called "the circumcised," done by hand in the
> flesh. At that time you were without the Messiah,
> excluded from the citizenship of Israel, and
> foreigners to the covenants of the promise, with no
> hope and without God in the world. But now in
> Christ Jesus, you who were far away have been
> brought near by the blood of the Messiah. For He is
> our peace, who made both groups one and tore down
> the dividing wall of hostility. In His flesh, He did
> away with the law of the commandments in regula-
> tions, so that He might create in Himself one new

man from the two, resulting in peace. [He did this so] that He might reconcile both to God in one body through the cross and put the hostility to death by it. When [Christ] came, He proclaimed the good news of peace to you who were far away and peace to those who were near. For through Him we both have access by one Spirit to the Father. So then you are no longer foreigners and strangers, but fellow citizens with the saints, and members of God's household, built on the foundation of the apostles and prophets, with Christ Jesus Himself as the cornerstone. The whole building is being fitted together in Him and is growing into a holy sanctuary in the Lord, in whom you also are being built together for God's dwelling in the Spirit. (Eph. 2:11–22)

Several phrases seem to have special application to Jews and Arabs today:

- "For He is our peace"
- "tore down the dividing wall of hostility"
- "one new man from the two, resulting in peace"
- "that He might reconcile both to God in one body through the cross"
- "For through Him we both have access by one Spirit to the Father."
- "growing into a holy sanctuary in the Lord"
- "being built together for God's dwelling in the Spirit"

The passage that God inspired the apostle Paul to write is about Jewish-Gentile barriers that have been collapsed all at once through the power of His cross. I don't mean to toss the context in the trash can, but look at these phrases and think about Jewish-Arab barriers instead. Imagine the joy in Yahweh's heart when the sons of Abraham, Isaac, and Ishmael reconcile—when Jew and Arab forgive each other. Ah, the beauty of it. The holiness of the moment covers over the centuries of rooted bitterness and washes it clean. It is one of the most noticeable reconciliation miracles among all people groups. The world's attention is continually captured by the strife and acidic hate of the Middle East. How many times is the lead news story direct from Israel another up-close picture of more bloody violence? But the power of the cross of Christ and the cleansing effect of His blood is the only blood that's needed to end the conflict.

During the Gulf War of the 1990s, evidence of wall crumbling began to circulate throughout churches in Israel. As in America, many churches seem to be separated along ethnic lines in Israel—Arab churches in one section of the city, Jewish messianic churches in another section. I believe that this grieves our Father's heart. The biggest praise session of all time is going to be the one in heaven in which people from every tribe and tongue worship our holy God together. So why can't we get started here? Well, during the war, a remarkable thing began to occur. Arab believers reached out to Jewish believers in the midst of Saddam's barrage of Scud missiles landing in Israel. The target city was Tel Aviv for three reasons:

1. Israel has a nuclear reactor in the Tel Aviv area. Saddam tried to bait the Israelis, knowing that if they jumped into the fray, other Arab nations would join his cause.
2. Tel Aviv is free of Muslim holy sites. So, if Saddam had fired away at Jerusalem and happened to accidently stick a missile through the Dome of the Rock or Al-Aqsa Mosque, the entire Muslim world would have descended on Baghdad to take out the Iraqi dictator.
3. Tel Aviv has the largest population in Israel, and, thus, the Butcher of Baghdad could have gotten more bang out of his bombs by aiming at the coastal city. Jewish people were understandably frightened and on edge

as soon as American troops entered Iraq. Saddam had promised to strike Israel if the United States struck Iraq. He made good on his promise, and, nightly, Israelis hid in their sealed rooms in anticipation of the next missile barrage. Some of the Jewish people who panicked the most were survivors of Nazi concentration camps. They were reminded of the painful past that they had survived and now faced again.

Arab believers went into action and reached out to comfort their hurting Israeli brothers and sisters. As they did, they put their own lives in danger as Saddam was catapulted to the number-one hero among Palestinians and even some Arab Israelis. In one instance, an Arab pastor living in the Arab section of East Jerusalem offered a Jewish family refuge in his own home. He called a Tel Aviv pastor and asked the pastor, his wife, and three daughters to come stay with him and his family. As the messianic pastor told me the story, I had tears in my eyes. If the Arab pastor had been caught with Jews in his house in the midst of Iraq's attack on Israel, who knows what would have happened? "One new man from the two, resulting in peace."

The Arab Mind-set Tethered to Islam

In his book *Circle of Fear*, Hussein Sumaida tells his story as an Israeli spy in Iraq. The cloak-and-dagger real-life thriller uncovers the thinking that oozes out of the Muslim world today.

In spite of the concentrated effort to turn every-one into America-haters, everyone continued to love American clothes, hamburgers, blue jeans, music, and the rest of the outer shell of American culture. At the same time, deep down, many had a genuine hatred of American global power. The reason for this can be explained in one word: Israel. It is a measure of the depth of the Arab's hatred for Israel that, even though they loved so much about American pop culture, when it came down to brass tacks, they viewed America as the enemy. America meant Israel. Anyone who fails to understand this will not understand why "the situation in the Middle East" cannot be solved. Because America is so intimately allied with Israel, and Israel is seen as the root of all evil in the Arab world, then whenever anything bad happens in the Arab world, it is the fault of the Americans. I don't say this as theory but as a fact. There is no intermediary analytical thought. My theory is my belief, therefore a fact.[1]

Only the power of Almighty God can give a new mind to a person who thinks like this. Only Jesus Christ can release a person from generational sin entrenchment that runs this deep. Arab people need release from thirteen centuries of Islamic enslavement.

The Jewish Mind-set Still Searching

At a Billy Graham crusade this year in Dallas, Texas, the preacher of the ages said that the last time he was in Jerusalem he enjoyed a visit with the chief rabbi of the Holy City. The rabbi remarked to Graham that Judaism and Christianity had much in common. Where the two parted company was over the person of the Messiah. "You believe the Messiah is Jesus and we're just not sure," the rabbi said. To which I would love to ask the rabbi if I ever meet him, "Well, how long is it going to take for you to make up your mind?" Actually, this is a major step forward for the leading Jewish rabbi to admit his searching with such candor. Often, Jesus is dismissed altogether, but God must be working in his heart to bring him to this point of openness. Why is it so hard for the Jews to receive their spiritual laser treatment and correct their eyesight once and for all? Because the time has not been right. The evidence has been written down in their own words. Jewish commentaries paint a picture of the Messiah that can only be Jesus. The Talmud and the Midrash are rabbinical interpretations of the Law, prophets, and writings. Their own pens led them on a trail through the centuries straight to Christ. Listen to the learned rabbis:

The Concept of the Messiah

"And as for the wonders that are not the work of Adonai, when he, that is the Messiah, comes then he will heal the sick, resurrect the dead, and to the poor announce glad tidings." (4Q521, Dead Sea Scrolls at Qumran)

"It was taught in the School of Elijah, the world will endure 6,000 years—2,000 years in chaos, 2,000 with Torah, and 2,000 years will be the days of the Messiah." (Babylonian Talmud, Sanhedrin 97a)

The Messiah to Appear in Israel

"The King Messiah . . . from where does he come forth? From the royal city of Bethlehem in Judah." (Jerusalem Talmud, Berakoth 5a)

"The Messiah . . . will arise in the land of Galilee. . . . the Messiah shall reveal himself in the land of Galilee because in this part of the Holy Land the desolation (Babylonian exile) first began, therefore he will manifest himself there first." (Zohar III, Shemoth 7b, 8b, 220a; Otzar Midrashim, 466)

The Messiah to Provide Atonement

"Rabbi Yochanan said, 'The Messiah—what is his name?' . . . And our Rabbis said, 'the pale one . . . is his name,' as it is written 'Surely he took up our infirmities and carried our sorrows—yet we considered him stricken by G-d, smitten by him and afflicted.'" (Babylonian Talmud, Sanhedrin 98, p. 2)

"The Messiah our righteousness has turned from us. We are alarmed, we have no one to justify us. Our sins and the yoke of our transgressions he bore. He was bruised for our iniquities. He carried on his shoulders our sins. With his stripes we are healed (Isa. 53). Almighty G-d, hasten the day that he might come to us anew; that we may hear from Mt. Lebanon (figurative reference to the Temple), a second time through the Messiah." (Ancient hymn-prayer by Eliezer Hakkallir sung during the Musaf Service on Yom Kippur; included in some *Siddurs* [which are prayer and hymn books Jews use on Friday evening].)

Recognizing the Messiah

"Prepare the way! The King Messiah comes. . . . may the mountains abase themselves, may the valleys be filled, may the cedars incline to render him homage. Prostrate yourselves all of you before the Messiah King, and bend your knees before him who is seated at the right hand of the Holy One." (Zohar I.4b)

"Now there was about this time, Yeshua (Eaysoos in Greek), a wise man, if it be lawful to call him a man, for he was a doer of wonderful works, a teacher of such men as receive the truth with pleasure. He drew over to him both many of the Jews and many of the Gentiles. He was Mashiach (Christos in Greek); and when Pilate, at the suggestion of the principal men amongst us, had condemned him to the cross, those that loved him at the first did not forsake him, for he appeared to them alive again the third day, as the divine prophets had foretold these and ten thousand other wonderful things concerning him; and the tribe of Christians (followers of Messiah), so named from him, are not extinct at this day." (*Antiquities of the Jews*, book 18, chapter 3, paragraph 3; Yosef ben Mattityahu, aka Josephus)

"Our Rabbis taught: during the last forty years before the destruction of the Temple, the lot for the L-rd (on Yom Kippur) did not come up in the right hand; nor did the crimson-colored strap become white (on the neck of the scapegoat); nor did the western-most light shine; and the doors of the Hekal (temple) would open by themselves." (Babylonian Talmud, Yoma, 39b)

The Hebrew expression *la chaim* means "to life." Steve Herzog explained its meaning this way: "Jewish people frequently wear gold charms depicting this Hebrew character on chains around their necks, emphasizing the fact that life is Judaism's most precious and cherished commodity."[2] Life is precious to Jews worldwide. They have experienced death so often; living the day to its fullest is the objective, but a tall order at that.

How ironic that life is what every Jew desires to live to the hilt. "I have come that they may have life and have it in abundance" (John 10:10). Jesus knew that locked in every Jewish heart was this innermost desire. No civilization of people has been more threatened throughout their history than the Jews. Nations have turned on them. Kings have attacked them. They have been the human punching bags of the ages. Satan has deceived even himself into thinking he could slaughter them for good. World rulers have made it their main objective and continue to today.

In junior high, upper-class bullies picked on me. I was so ridiculed at one point that I decided to fight back. I wasn't going to take it anymore! My Irish blood was boiling—watch it buddy! Unfortunately, the day I got guts was the day that Steven Custer picked on me. He was roughly two and a half times my size. I was losing until my older sister, Terry, intervened. I hated being picked on. Israel has experienced this from day one. Its birth as a nation came at the end of four hundred years of slavery in Egypt. Oppression? The Israelis have had it! Genocide? Attempted first on them. Ruled over in their own country? Let's see . . . the Romans, the Mamluks, the Turks, the . . . oh, that's enough. Israel has been the continual victim of the world's bullies. Everyone has gone after them. It's almost as if a nation can't be on the who's-who list unless somewhere on its agenda is the liquidation of Israel. Does anybody out there not find this a little over the top?

That's why we, the church, must bring life to Israel. That's a powerful message for the Jews—when so many would like to bring death to them, we offer life. Any Jewish person values life.

Just Do It!

What is Israel's future as far as God's plan goes? Robert Thomas answered this beautifully.

Old Testament Messianic prophecies begin as early as Genesis 3:15, a verse that depicts the Messiah's mission of bruising the serpent's head. It was some time before revelation of the mission of Israel, however. That awaited the call of Abraham (Genesis 12:1–3). From that point on, the mission of Israel paralleled that of the Messiah in many ways. Why did God single out Abraham and his descendants from the rest of mankind? It was His chosen method of dealing with humans as a whole to limit His special attention to one segment of them. He gave this segment of people a mission to the rest of the world so that He could fulfill through them His ultimate mission for all people. In light of Israel's failings along the way, the Messiah has filled and will fill the gap in redeeming Israel so that Israel can eventually fulfill her responsibility to the rest of the world.[3]

Thomas went on to say that the ultimate goal of the Messiah and Israel is to bring glory to God. I would add that is the ultimate goal of the church as well. The God of Israel displays His concise, consistently planned outcomes in Scripture this way:

God's Bottom Line

- The Messiah: "Glorify Your Son so that the Son may glorify You" (John 17:1b).
- Israel: "Rejoice, heavens, for the LORD has acted; shout, depths of the earth. Break out into singing, mountains, forest, and every tree in it. For the LORD has redeemed Jacob, and glorifies Himself through Israel" (Isa. 44:23).
- The church: "In Him we were also made His inheritance, predestined according to the purpose of the One who works out everything in agreement with the decision of His will, so that we who had already put our hope in the Messiah might bring praise to His glory" (Eph. 1:11–12).

OK, it's a clean sweep. The Messiah, the nation of Israel, and the church are God's primary vehicles to bring Him glory. So clear. So pristine is this eternal objective with God. The apostle Paul said that because this is the spiritual priority one it ought to permeate every phase of our loving no matter how big or small. "Therefore, whether you eat or drink, or whatever you do, do everything for God's glory" (1 Cor. 10:31).

The Messiah, Israel, and the church have all been called to glorify. The pursuit of this is much like climbing a large mountain. Jesus was, of course, the first to arrive at the summit.

The church is in the midst of its climb. Israel got lost along the way. How can Israel bring glory to Almighty God in its present state of rejecting the Messiah? They cannot. The questions are: Can we, the church, do anything about it? Can we give a hand to God's chosen people who collectively have made the biggest mistake in all of history? (They went the wrong direction.) Can we expect a spiritual U-turn? I believe so, and here's how we, the church, can help Israel all "for the praise of His glory."

Get Out the Sackcloth and Ashes

Thomas Cahill, writer of *How the Irish Saved Civilization*, also penned another best-seller entitled *The Gift of the Jews: How a Tribe of Desert Nomads Changed the Way Everyone Thinks and Feels.* Cahill flatly rejects biblical inspiration. In his eyes, anyone who upholds the belief is delusional. Nevertheless, surprisingly he made some insightful deductions about Jews worldwide: "Our history is replete with examples of those who have refused to see what the Jews are really about, who—through intellectual blindness, racial chauvinism, xenophobia, or just plain evil—have been able to give this oddball tribe, this raggle-taggle band, this race of wanderers who are the progenitors of the western world, their due. Indeed, at the end of the bloodiest of centuries, we can all too easily look back on scenes of unthinkable horror perpetrated by those who would do anything rather than give the Jews their due."[4] I agree. Unfortunately, our entire church history has been caught up in this type of thinking too. Jews have been misunderstood by us Christians. We still see deep pockets of anti-Semitism within the church.

In John Hagee's book *Final Dawn over Jerusalem,* he grimly recounted how the Nazi agenda was extracted from the church's treatment of the Jews throughout history. Buckle your seat belts; the ride is rough.

Roman Church Policy

1. Prohibition of intermarriage and of sexual intercourse between Christians and Jews, Synod of Elvira, AD 306.

2. Jews and Christians not permitted to eat together, Synod of Elvira, AD 306.

3. Jews not allowed to hold public office, Synod of Clermont, AD 535. Also Fourth Lateran Council, 1215.

4. Jews not allowed to employ Christian servants or possess Christian slaves, Third Synod of Orleans, AD 538.

5. Jews not permitted to show themselves in the streets during Passion Week, Third Synod of Orleans, AD 538.

6. Burning of the Talmud and other books, Twelfth Synod of Toledo, AD 681.

7. Christians not permitted to patronize Jewish doctors, Trulanic Synod, AD 692.

8. Jews obligated to pay taxes for support of the church to the same extent as Christians, Fourth Lateran Council, 1215.

9. Jews not permitted to be plaintiffs or witnesses against Christians in the courts, Third Lateran Council, 1179.

10. Jews not permitted to withhold inheritance from descendants who had accepted Christianity, Third Lateran Council, 1179.

11. Jews must wear a distinctive badge, Fourth Lateran Council, 1215.

12. Construction of new synagogues prohibited, Council of Oxford, 1222.

13. Christians not permitted to attend Jewish ceremonies, Synod of Vienna, 1267.

14. Jews forced to live in ghettos away from Christians, Synod of Breslau, 1267.

15. Jews not permitted to obtain academic degrees, Council of Basel, 1434.

16. Mass extermination of the Jews in the Crusades. Fourth Lateran Council called upon secular powers to "exterminate all heretics," 1215. The Inquisition burned Jews at the stake while confiscating their property, 1478.

Nazi Policy

1. Law for the Protection of German Blood and Honor, September 15, 1935.

2. Jews barred from dining cars, December 30, 1939.

3. Law for Re-Establishment of the Professional Civil Service, April 7, 1935, by which Jews were expelled from office and civil service jobs.

4. Law for the Protection of German Blood and Honor, September 15, 1935, forbade Germans from hiring Jews.

5. Decree authorizing local authorities to bar Jews from the streets on certain days (Nazi holidays), December 3, 1938.

6. Nazi book burnings in Germany.

7. Decree of July 25, 1938, forbidding Germans from patronizing Jewish doctors.

8. Jews to pay a special tax in lieu of donations for party purposes imposed on Nazis, December 24, 1940.

9. Jews not permitted to institute civil suits.

10. Decree empowering the Justice Ministry to void wills offending the "sound judgment of the people," July 31, 1938.

11. Decree forcing all Jews to wear the yellow Star of David, September 1, 1941.

12. Destruction of synagogues in entire Reich, November 10, 1938. The Jews refer to this night as Kristallnacht.

13. Friendly relations with Jews prohibited, October 24, 1941.

14. Jews forced to live in ghettos, order of Heydrich, September 21, 1939.

15. All Jews expelled from schools and universities throughout the Third Reich with the Law against Overcrowding of German Schools and Universities, April 25, 1933.

16. Hitler's Final Solution called for the systematic slaughter of every Jew in Europe. He took their homes, their jobs, their possessions (even the gold fillings in their teeth), and finally, their lives. His justification? "It's the will of God and the work of the Church."[5]

First, how could this have taken place? The early church fathers clearly got us off to a terrible start in our treatment of Jews. As the leaders go, so goes the church. If I had to single out the worst example of anti-Semitism within the church, it would be John Chrysostom. He was born in the place believers were first called Christians about AD 350. He became a bishop of Constantinople and a major church influencer regarding Jewish treatment. He was the prince of preachers of the fourth century and wrote extensively. He is hailed as a church hero for his unwavering commitment to Christ. His legacy is one of excellence in application of the Scriptures from the Greek Bible. His sermons have survived and are still read 1,600 years later. Known as the "golden mouth," he was the first in a long line of gifted communicators of the Word of God. His views on the Jewish people, however, need to be repudiated once and for all.

David Dolan recorded these incriminating words:

Father Flannery cites many other instances of growing hostility toward the Jews by early church fathers. This hostility reached its height in the sermons and writings of John Chrysostom (AD 344–407). According to Flannery, Chrysostom "stands without peer or parallel in the virulence of his attack." He quotes from eight sermons by Chrysostom—the most popular preacher of the fourth century—in which this preacher called the Jews "lustful, rapacious, greedy, perfidious bandits, inveterate murders, destroyers, men possessed by the devil" with the "manners of the pig and the lusty goat." Jews "worship the devil," and their religion is "a disease." They have fallen into such a state because of their "odious assassination of Christ." Therefore, God hates the Jews, who will always remain without the temple or a sovereign nation. If all of this did not lead to obvious conclusions among

his Christian audience, Chrysostom spelled it out
even more explicitly for them, calling for a perpetual
Christian "holy war" against the Jews: "He who can
never love Christ enough will never have done with
fighting against those who hate Him."[6]

As the church continued to walk in this error, only a few
reasons can explain this position:

- Racism: Hatred of Jews because of their religion. This
  doesn't wash since Jesus, the prophets, the apostles,
  and first church leaders were all Jewish.

- Ignorance: Could the church have been only moder-
  ately guilty because we were in the dark about God's
  plan for His chosen people? No excuses; it's throughout the Bible. The New Testament clearly presents the
  fact that God is not finished with the Jews.

- Jealousy: Are Christians guilty of being jealous of God's
  relationship with Isaac's descendants? This doesn't
  square either because Romans 10:19 tells us God will
  make Israel jealous of the Gentiles not vice versa.

- Replacement: This view is akin to theological suicide
  for it falsely asserts that God is done with Israel. In
  this view, we, the church, take the Jews' place and
  even receive their promises now. It is not only arrogant but throws a literal interpretation of God's Word
  out the window.

- Deception: Satan has a personal agenda to convince
  the world that Jews are to be blamed for every problem known to humanity. The father of lies has done a
  superb job of this; apparently he has even convinced
  some believers too.

It's time to conduct the funeral and to pronounce that
Christian anti-Semitism is dead and will not be resurrected.
Anytime we take the same stand on an issue as the world does,
that ought to tell us something.

We must repent of this ongoing evil and seek God's forgiveness. We must be moved with compassion as Jesus was. He wept for Jerusalem as He was overlooking the city. Pray that God opens your spirit to have the same heart for Jews as He does. The church is held back in its mission as a result of this evil heresy. Yes, I have strong feelings about this. I am guilty too. I have judged, condemned, and laughed at Jewish people myself. I'm sure this broke God's heart. Would you join me in praying for forgiveness? *Holy God, the God of Israel, I ask You to forgive me when it comes to my thoughts, actions, and words against the people You chose to bring glory to Your name. I have been unfair to Jewish people, and I repent. I commit to turn away from this evil. I pray Your Holy Spirit will convict me if I fall for this trap of Satan again. I love Your people. Please give me Your love for them. I also ask that You place in me a passion to reach them for Jesus. I want them to be saved. Apart from Christ, I know they have no chance. Break my heart over this, Lord. Use me to reach Jewish people, I ask. Send me, Lord.*

We must admit the truth. Let's be honest. We have blown it, believers. I dare you to ask a Jewish person for forgiveness. You will not believe what that does to your spirit. I know. I've done it. It is healing. We need it and so do they. My wife, JoAnn, and a few of our kids were at a movie called *Remember the Titans*. The movie was a favorite for jocks, but there was a strong message of racial reconciliation. My wife was constantly reminded of the tension between blacks and whites in America throughout the movie because she was sitting next to a woman who was black. After the credits rolled by, JoAnn couldn't stand the conviction any longer. She said to the woman, "I am so sorry for what you and your family have probably experienced as far as racism in your lives. I just want to ask you if you would please forgive me for all the discrimination and grief that you have gone through as a result of bigotry shown to you by white people." The woman hugged my wife and said, "First of all, thank you!" And then she went on to say, "I do forgive you."

I know, some of you will no doubt be saying when it comes to Jewish people, "I've never uttered an anti-Semitic remark in my life." Well, then, when others have, did you stand up and defend God's covenant people? Neither have I. That's why I have asked them to forgive me. I want them to know that I recognize how wrong this is. I tell them that Christians are changing, and we do want to be their friends.

In Israel recently an Arab-Israeli pastors' meeting in Jerusalem was visited by the presence of God. As the clergymen were discussing how they could better coordinate and be more effective, the God who dwelled on the Temple Mount for centuries descended in power. An Arab pastor "broke the ice" by getting on his knees before the Jewish pastors. He asked them to forgive him and his people. He told the messianic pastors that his people had been guilty of bitterness and hatred of Jews for centuries. "Forgive us for all of the things we've done to you and for how much you have suffered on account of us, the Arab people." In a moment, all of the Arab pastors were on their knees, seeking forgiveness also. The Jewish pastors fell to their knees and likewise asked for forgiveness. "We have hated your people, too; we are just as guilty." No one wanted to go home. Yahweh was there, and His presence was sweet. Isaac and Ishmael embraced each other that day in Jerusalem. Ah yes, after 4,100 years of conflict . . . it was about time, don't you think?

It's been 1,970 years for the conflict between Christians and Jews. It's about time to end it. Let's ask God's forgiveness. Let's ask their forgiveness. Let's go on.

Until we face the truth and do something about it, we have little chance of befriending Jews and leading them to their awaiting Jewish Messiah. This will bring our Father much glory. When we reach out to the lost sheep of Israel, we truly are following Jesus.

What about Ishmael's Descendants?

I hope by now you have a new sense of passion for Jews. What about Arabs, though? Are you moved with compassion for them? I wasn't for a long time. When one goes to Israel, it's easy to relate to the Jews because of our common roots. It's also easy to forget about Arabs altogether.

Abraham, of course, had Ishmael before he had Isaac. Ishmael was thirteen years old, in fact, before Isaac arrived. In amazing irony, the angel of the Lord is the one who reached out to Hagar, the slave woman who bore Ishmael for Abraham. Abraham's wife, Sarah, had started to panic because she was now old and still not pregnant. She tried to fulfill God's promise of a descendant her way. When Hagar slept with Abraham at Sarah's request, she became pregnant. Sarah then had second thoughts. In the midst of an emotional overflow, Sarah cruelly sent Hagar away. It was the angel of the Lord who searched for Hagar.

Why do I find this ironic? Because Muslims today believe that they are descendants of Ishmael. This admittedly is debatable. Yet they believe it strongly. Who was the one who reached out to Hagar with compassion and "found" her? It was Jesus. Jesus is the Angel of the Lord of the Old Testament. We know this because characteristics of God's nature are seen in *the* Angel of the Lord. They are not seen in other angels of the Lord. Only the Angel of the Lord. In Genesis 16:9, the Angel of the Lord promised that he would increase Hagar's descendants and that they would become too numerous to count. A mere angel would not make this promise because he would be incapable of delivering on it. Only God could do this. This was a pre-New Testament encounter with Christ.

Therefore, it was Jesus who showed the first act of compassion and kindness for the mother of Ishmael. Muslims believe they are directly linked to this son of Abraham, but if it hadn't been for Jesus, he probably wouldn't have made it to birth. His mother would have had great difficulty surviving and giving birth in the desert between Israel and Egypt. Jesus Himself told Hagar to go back to Abraham. She bore Ishmael, which in Hebrew means "God hears." He had heard a desperate mother's cry, searched for her, made her a promise of many descendants, and brought her back to safety.

The happy home was soon in chaos again. Hagar foolishly mocked Sarah at a feast in honor of Isaac. Hagar was again banished to the desert, this time with Ishmael, now a teenager. But the water was soon gone, and Hagar began to sob. This time her son joined her. The Angel of the Lord came to the rescue again. This time the Angel of the Lord called to Hagar from heaven. He said that Ishmael had called out His name, and God had heard him crying. God was moved. He promised Hagar that not only would Ishmael survive but he would flourish into a great nation. He next met their obvious physical needs and opened her eyes to show her a well of water for her thirsty boy.

Jesus:

- heard Hagar crying and responded in love.
- brought her out of the harsh desert back to Abraham to have a safe birth.
- was not finished with her, even though Hagar brought on her second banishment from Abraham.
- again heard her cries and her son's also. He was moved.
- promised to make Ishmael into a great nation. This must have been a little hard to comprehend for Hagar, who believed Ishmael was close to death.
- met their needs with water.

Genesis 21 goes on to say that God was with Ishmael. He was raised in the desert and later united with half-brother Isaac to bury their father Abraham in Hebron. Abraham did leave everything he owned to Isaac. Make no mistake about it, the Abrahamic blessing was transferable through Isaac not

Ishmael. Yet none other than Jesus Christ Himself intervened on behalf of the future great nation.

This is amazing to me. If Muslims are descendants of Ishmael, then they have Jesus to thank because of it. Without Jesus, they wouldn't be here. Arabs who are Ishmael's offspring would be gone also. Muslims have never thanked Jesus. Instead, they have tried to destroy His church.

The Angel of the Lord, Jesus, had compassion on Ishmael. I believe we should also since the Arab people are enveloped in the false religion of Islam. I believe we should start there. We must bring them Jesus. They are reachable. That seems like a good place to begin. When President Bush said that terrorists had hijacked the religion of Islam, I thought about those words for awhile. I think Islam has hijacked the entire Arab culture!

The Angel of the Lord prophetically laid out the "way of Ishmael" in Genesis 16:11–12: "You have conceived and will have a son. You will name him Ishmael, for the LORD has heard your [cry of] affliction. This man will be [like] a wild ass. His hand will be against everyone, and everyone's hand will be against him; he will live at odds with all his brothers."

Whoa, was Jesus ever right! Arabs are famous for their conflict within their enormous family ranks. People often ask me, "How have the Jews survived living among Arabs that outnumber them ten to one?" I say two things:

1. The Abrahamic covenant given to Israel from God.
2. The Arabs fight with each other as much as they do with Jews. Their hostility toward each other has kept them from solidarity.

One of the gems I remember from a seminary professor was: "It's not hard to find what Satan's up to; just look at what God's doing, and Satan's trying to undo it." Simple but true. God said that Ishmael's descendants would be a fractured family. Satan has tried to bring them together. The vehicle he has used is the religion of Islam.

Muhammad, I believe, was severely demonized. His visions of "Allah" threw him into seizures that certainly didn't originate in heaven. They were bizarre to say the least. In the classic work *The Story of Islam*, Theodore Lunt writes, "The visitations occurred several times, and each time they were accompanied by violent physical effects upon Mohammed. He was angry if anyone looked at him: his face was covered with foam, his eyes were closed, and sometimes he roared like a camel."[7] He murdered. He had numerous wives. His last one was nine years old. He controlled women. Islam allows four wives. Muhammad had as many as he wanted. Of course, this was his privilege since he was a prophet of God. How convenient! How a woman can ever remain Muslim after she has read the Koran is beyond me. Muhammad made the following declarations about women:[8]

- They are the majority of the people in hell.
- They lack intelligence.
- They lack faith.
- They possess sinister characters.
- They can have only one-half of the man's rightful inheritance.
- If a woman walks in front of a man while he is praying, the prayer is no good and has to be said over. (This is also true if a donkey or a dog does the same thing. This declaration really amazes me.)

Don McCurry in his fine work titled *Healing the Broken Family of Abraham* compared Muhammad with Jesus (see next page). It is illuminating.

But Satan's blinding of Muslims is powerful. Only Jesus can open their eyes. And He is doing that as a tidal wave of conversions to Christ is sweeping across the Muslim world. Muslims have a new openness to Jesus. The growing "negatives" emanating from their religion have catapulted even devout Muslims into a spiritual quest. It can only be explained

Muhammad	Christ
Reflected the qualities of a seventh-century Arab man	Reflected the image of God
Instituted holy war in God's name	Taught disciples not to fight
Institutionalized looting of war victims	Warned against covetousness
Taught vengeance	Taught forgiveness
Legalized polygamy and concubinage	Upheld ideal of monogamy
Demeaned the role of women	Honored women
Made divorce easy for men but not for women	Spoke against divorce
Taught sensuous view of paradise	Indicated an afterlife on a higher plane in presence of the Father
Institutionalized Arabic Middle Eastern rituals of religious duties	Taught that true worship was in Spirit and truth
Advocated once-in-a lifetime pilgrimage to Mecca	Taught that we are life-long pilgrims in this world
Substituted his law for Mosaic Law	Fulfilled Mosaic Law in love
Ignored the need for blood sacrifice for sins	Came to give His life, shed His blood for the sins of others
Maintained atonement for sins was not possible	Came to make atonement for our sins
Denied the Crucifixion	His life culminated in crucifixion and resurrection and ascension
Had no power over Satan or demons	Broke Satan's power in life and at the cross
Had no power to give his disciples	Gave His disciples power and authority over demons
Assumed Islam was the expression of the kingdom of God	Introduced the kingdom of God and Himself as King
Reduced Jesus to being a prophet for his age only	Jesus was the culmination of offices of Prophet, Priest, and King for all time
He cursed those who thought Jesus was the Son of God	Jesus said he who honors the Son honors the Father
No concept of God as our Father	Came to bring us back to our heavenly Father
Confessed he could do no miracles	Attested to the presence of the kingdom with his miracles
Died	Died and then rose from the dead[9]

this way: God has orchestrated a major revival among Muslims. They are giving Jesus a second, third, and fourth look. The gospel is hitting home with them because their religious system has no sacrifice to pay for their sins. They are beginning to understand the need for a Savior.

McCurry continued in his book with a salute to the first Protestant missionary to Muslims, Henry Martyn. Martyn is known for having said he wanted "to burn out for God." A learned man, he could speak Urdu, Persian, Arabic, and Sanskrit. He was trained at Cambridge University. Although he died at thirty-two, he became the "fireball for God" he hoped to be. He was not only a missionary. He translated the New Testament in three languages, one of which was Arabic. He wrote tracts. He debated Muslims. He developed seven principles for working with Muslims. Two hundred years later, they are still effective:

Martyn's seven principles to reach Muslims

1. Share your own personal experience—your testimony of how you experienced the forgiveness of sins and peace with God through Jesus Christ.

2. Appreciate the best in your Muslim friend and ascribe such qualities to God working in his life. The same could go for those elements in Muslim culture that are genuinely approved by God.

3. Keep your message Christ-centered, as you talk about the grace of God and how it is mediated through Christ and carried forward by the sanctifying work of God's Spirit.

4. Draw your Muslim friend into the study of the Scriptures so that he can discover these new truths for himself.

5. Play the role of a supporting friend as your Muslim friend goes through this time of critical investigation and decision-making.

6. Create a favorable atmosphere in society by ministering to human needs.

7. Trust the Holy Spirit to work in your Muslim friend as he seeks his place as a believer in his Muslim context.[10]

Whether Muslims are descendants of Ishmael is not all that important. We must reach out to them as the Angel of the Lord did to Ishmael when he was near death in the desert. Jesus' perfect love for people demands that we pursue them as He does. No one is outside of the far-reaching hand of God. No one is. This is the time, believers. The harvest is ripe.

Expect a Miracle Today

At EvangeCube, "expect a miracle today" is a ministry phrase that we try to live by. Nowhere have I seen those words realized more than in Israel and in the Middle East. God is so vigorously pursing Jews and Muslims that seeing the miraculous is normal there.

In this chapter we've seen that even though Jewish unbelief and Arabic ties to Islam are formidable foes, they can be overcome. More prayer is being laser-beamed toward Israel than at any other time. Jesus has awakened His bride to intercession, fasting, prayer walking, and prayer for the nations. Christians from various parts of the world travel thousands of miles to Israel for the sole purpose of "praying on location." Healing between Arabs and Jews is happening within the body of Christ. Both groups are burdened for each other. God is replacing the enmity between the descendants of Abraham with genuine affection and biblical reconciliation. Not only are Arab and messianic pastors praying together; they are exchanging pulpits. Walls of separation are falling. Centuries of mistrust are evaporating. The church is triumphing again in the land in which it was born:

- In Jerusalem, a messianic church prays for the Arab church in the Gaza Strip.
- A prayer meeting in the Holy City meets weekly now with hundreds of Arab and Jewish believers praying as one.

- A wounded Palestinian from Bethlehem was given an Israeli soldier's identification card so he could travel to Jerusalem for an operation that saved his life.
- In a Tel Aviv rehabilitation center, Jewish believers wheelchair-danced with an Arab soldier from Lebanon who lost both of his legs in a war with Israel. His Jewish friends are family now.
- In Ramallah, a desperate Palestinian woman pleaded with Israeli soldiers to let her through closed checkpoints and into a Jerusalem hospital. Her son was dying. He not only now lives, but the woman received no bill for the expensive surgery and hospital stay.
- Life-giving churches of Israel, Jordan, Egypt, Syria, Iraq, and other Middle East countries are experiencing significant growth in the midst of unstable times.
- A saint of God smuggles Bibles into Saudi Arabia by packing them in the tires of his car.
- An American soldier preaches at a local Baghdad church after the Iraq war. The Iraqis welcome him with open arms. He is followed by an Arab believer from Jordan who trains the Iraqis in the EvangeCube so they can begin an outreach campaign in Saddam's former capital city.

Traveling the United Arab Emirates, our mission team was warned that if we were caught with EvangeCubes, they would be confiscated, and we would be sent out of the country immediately. Pete Pintus, Allen Reedall, Jay Straub, and I entered with more than one thousand of them in our suitcases. The churches of the United Arab Emirates prayed and fasted the whole day and pleaded for a miracle. They got one. We were there to see it. An official tore through our bags and quickly found the cubes.

The EvangeCube is a visual presentation of the gospel and an excellent cross-cultural tool because it is all pictures and told as a story. It has six pictures that vividly communicate Christ's death, burial, and resurrection. It truly is anointed by God. We were told ahead of our arrival that picture 2 would be the big problem to the Muslim guards at the airport. You see, the second picture is of Jesus dying on the cross. A definite no-no in the world of Islam. Muslims believe Jesus existed and even was a prophet; however, they stop there. Jesus as an atoning Savior and Lamb of God who died for our sins is to Muslims a figment of our Christian imaginations. A picture of Jesus on the cross can send an observant Muslim "into orbit." Within minutes, four guards were taking EvangeCubes out of the boxes as fast as they could.

Then God did a miracle before our eyes. He kept the guards from ever seeing Jesus on the cross. For twenty minutes they turned the cubes every which way. Every time they missed seeing Jesus on the cross! Every time! As a result, about one thousand believers were trained how to effectively share their faith and are evangelizing this Muslim country. Jesus made the blind man see. He did the reverse on the guards. He made the seeing men blind. Hallelujah!

I close with this. Serving Christ in Israel or in the Middle East is not for the faint of heart. It is dangerous because Satan is losing ground fast, and he is on the prowl trying to devour the church. He will lose, of course, but he will attempt to intimidate the church through persecution and even martyrdom. Arabs and Jews are experiencing *musahala*, Arabic for "reconciliation." Satan cannot explain this since Islam says that it is impossible. Our holy God is pulling the church together, strengthening it, and sealing the evil one's fate all at once. Would we expect the deceiver of nations to go down without a fight? I don't think so. That's why serving Christ in the Middle East is so dynamic and thrilling. These are the front lines of God's kingdom advancing into darkness and shining God's light.

For us believers, it doesn't get any better than this. How privileged we are to live in this generation! Since the first century, there has not been a revival in Jerusalem or Israel or the entire Middle East like this.

This is classic spiritual warfare. Your help is needed. Even though we are winning, the battle rages. In chapter 8 we will find out where you fit into all of this. You have an assignment. Lives are hanging in the balance. All hands on deck, believer.

★ ✡ ★ ✡

Rima—The Life-Giver

THE SPIRITUAL BAROMETRIC pressure is rising in the Gaza Strip. A string of suicide bombings and border conflicts have resulted in closing all entrances into Israel. No one goes in; no one goes out. The Palestinian workforce is grounded for the week. There will be no one bringing in extra food, supplies, or paychecks. Lockdown is here again. At night, it's hard to sleep with the drone planes patrolling and watching. Because Gaza City is home to some of the worst terrorist groups in the Middle East, this is where Israel makes lightning-fast strikes to settle the score. Once the terrorists strike the Jewish innocents, the Israeli Defense Forces almost always make a move into Gaza. After the drone planes locate the guilty, Apache helicopters arrive to dispense retaliation. With precise accuracy, they fire and take out another terrorist mastermind. There are many more within the city's confines. The believers want the terrorists gone also. Their lives are being controlled by them. This is no way to live. How do people keep from losing their minds here? Missiles, machine-gun fire, and mass demonstrations occur on a daily basis. Children are raised in Gaza. Can you imagine a childhood in this pressure cooker?

Rima's home seems to be in another hemisphere—or at least another time zone. It is completely detached from the rage in the street below. There is life here. With death and suicide all around, this is a spiritual oasis. Rima and her husband minister in the name of Jesus and in the power of the Spirit in this place. She is a true life-giver. Her spiritual gifts are hospitality, encouragement, and teaching. She is a discipler of women. They are drawn to her. What wisdom she passed on to the young married women and the engaged!

Rima is one of the best cooks anywhere. Believers enjoy delicious meals daily from Rima's kitchen. It's as if there is an unlimited food supply in the Gaza Strip. When you're served at Rima's, the food keeps coming. Fresh fish, chicken tabouli, baba ganoush, hummus, and endless pita bread for Arabia-style dining. When I first met Rima, she cooked for about thirty people. The apartment is very small, and the kitchen has a tiny electric stove with two burners. Rima often cooks the night before and all day to have enough to serve her guests. I believe she feeds more people of Gaza than the United Nations does. She is one amazing woman.

But with Rima, food is another creative vehicle for ministry. What happens around the table for hours at a time is what it's all about. Gaza is a dangerous place. Somehow it all goes away at Rima's. In the Old Testament, the Lord established cities of refuge for criminals to find safety. In Gaza, it's just the opposite. Rima's home is a place to which the innocent flee. Jesus is lifted up here. Prayer meetings last into the early hours of the morning. The praise sessions are beautiful and impacting. Jesus is so real here. Believers often arrive tired, frustrated, and on edge due to the conflict everywhere they look. If they are from Muslim families and have escaped to become followers of Jesus, they find safe passage here. If they are unable to feed themselves due to the latest city lockdown, they are fed until stuffed here. The believers of the area receive a spiritual booster shot at Rima's.

Rima is an amazing woman in that she and her husband did not have a passion in their hearts to reach Muslims for Christ until only a few years ago. Previously, they avoided Muhammad's followers, preferring to labor in Christian areas. God performed a double bypass operation on the couple. He bypassed both of their hearts and gave them His heart for Muslims. They now overflow with passion to reach them with Christ. Their church has experienced steady growth each year since they arrived.

Many of the women Rima disciples will be pastors' wives someday. With church planting on the horizon, these women will be the Rimas of tomorrow. They will be life-givers, too, someday. Rima provides so much for the people of Gaza. She is a hero for Christ on this front line. When you enter the Gaza Strip for the first time, you are immediately struck by the hordes of people. They are packed into a small space for such a large city. This contributes to the oppressive feel of the area. The spiritual warfare is so intense here it is not uncommon for believers to get sick shortly after they arrive in Gaza.

The fruit of the Spirit is on display in Rima's home. It is a magnet to Gazans. In this city, there is a church building on a main street. It is the only evangelical one in Gaza City. One church for 1.5 million people. Rima serves them and combines a Martha work ethic with a Mary heart for God. She is making a difference for Jesus Christ in the place where suicide bombers grab the headlines. But Rima wields more influence, and hers will last all the way into an eternity.

★ ✡ ★ ✡

"Many women are capable, but you surpass them all!"
Charm is deceptive and beauty is fleeting, but a woman
who fears the LORD will be praised. Give her the reward of
her labor, and let her works praise her at the city gates.
PROVERBS 31:29–31

Chapter 8

Global Praying That Is Truly Biblical

What's needed in a hurry is a strategy for intercession
to maximize the moment in Israel and in the Middle East.
Intensive prayer movements are fueling the revival that
the region is now enjoying. Want to sign up?

Smoking for Jesus

To our mission team it was surprisingly hot for January in
Israel. Our day had been filled with ministry in Nazareth, and
we were due in Amman, Jordan, in a few hours to train a
Nazarene Church in how to share its faith, using the
EvangeCube. We were running late. Going into Jordan through
the Sheik Hussein bridge is normally an easy route into the
Hashemite kingdom, but today it was backed up. Would we
arrive for the church service on time? Jordanians and Iraqis
were waiting for us.

After long waits, our group of fourteen was almost through
until we hit security. That's where the trouble began. Carrying
about 1,200 EvangeCubes, we prayed that the guards would
scan only a few lead bags and then send us through. We were
told to proceed, and we were out of the doors when one of the
guards looking through the last bag spotted something. He said,
"Wait a minute." Since I was the leader of the mission group, I
was asked to accompany one of the guards into a room alone for
some questions. I walked into a small office, and six Jordanian
men were also sitting and waiting. All six were smoking.

The leader of security was sitting behind the desk, and he was angry. The guards had seen the picture on the cube of Jesus on the cross, and he held it up to me. He slapped the picture with the back of his hand, and we held this conversation:

Guard: "We don't want these in Jordan! These are not allowed here!"

Tom: "I've been to Jordan before, and we were able to bring EvangeCubes in. Did the rules change?"

Guard: "We don't want these in Jordan!"

Tom: "This is my fifth time to Jordan, and I love your country!" (Feeble attempt at schmoozing!)

Guard: "We don't like your president either! George Bush should not start a war with Iraq. If he wants to fight someone, why doesn't he go after North Korea?"

Tom: (I wanted to say, "Actually, I think they're next in line," but I figured that would score zero points), so I said, "I'm sorry you feel that way!"

There was an awkward silence. All six men were looking at me. I guess it was still my move. At that moment, the interrogator lit up a cigarette and handed it to me. I took it. I'm not sure why; I was never a smoker. Yeah, I tried a cigar in junior high but got real sick. Haven't touched tobacco since. Until now! I sat there with the cigarette ash getting longer and longer; I didn't smoke it. Finally, the ashes were falling off, and the angry questioner asked me one more question.

Guard: "Do you smoke?"

Tom: "No, I don't."

He started to laugh at me, that I had taken the cigarette but didn't smoke. All six men were laughing, and in an instant all the tension was out of the air. I felt I could breathe in there again, even with all the smoke!

Guard: "OK, we will let you in with these this time. It will cost you four hundred dollars."

Tom: "That's a little steep. How about two hundred?"

Guard: "How about four hundred dollars!"

Tom: "OK!"

It was worth a try, right? Praise God, we were through and on our way to the church in Amman. We arrived just after the service had begun. That night the worship was passionate and sweet. I didn't see any dry eyes in the house as Jordanians, Iraqis, and Americans lifted Jesus up high over Jordan. We arrived in time, so did the cubes, and approximately 190 people were sent on their way to share their faith throughout Jordan and Iraq. God turned a tense situation into one filled with laughter. One of those six guards as I left the border asked for an EvangeCube. Who knows how God will use that one.

Someone has said that taking the gospel into a foreign country is an act of spiritual warfare. Satan will retaliate when we advance into one of his strongholds. Therefore, it's very common at international borders to encounter resistance. Often we have found that team members may suddenly get sick or may get agitated with each other. All of this can happen upon entrance to a nation where there is a strong aversion to the gospel. This is understandable in Muslim-dominated countries. Satan has strong-armed them and controlled them for several centuries.

Prayer—The Slender Vein That Moves the Hand of God

Prayer is of utmost importance for missions advancement worldwide. The area from ten to forty degrees north of the equator, called the 10-40 window, is the home of the least evangelized people globally. Spiritual breakthroughs are starting to occur as a result of intensive prayer strategies in this area. The chains are stronger, tighter, and historical footholds that must be broken. Prayer is the precursor to God's hand moving.

I believe that the church took a turn for the better in the 1990s. Prayer groups for Israel began springing up in various places, and they all had one thing in common—fervency. The God of Israel began to burden His church for Jews, for Arabs, and for their tenuous situation. Up until then, gains for Christ had been very modest. I believe this was a turn for the better since we, the body of Christ, began to fall on our knees in anguish over Israel's present plight and the difficult days ahead.

In many churches I have been acquainted with, Israel is merely a major point in the overall study of eschatology. As I said previously, it felt as if we Christians used Israel. The Jews are back in the land, so Jesus' return must be around the corner. To put it bluntly, there should be more prayer going on for Israel and less prophecy. I have no problem with the study of prophecy. It is exciting to see the plan of God moving forward at this pace. I will be doing a prophecy conference this fall myself. But we need action, folks. We can no longer sit by and merely put check marks by our prophesies-fulfilled lists. We cannot remain idle. If we do, we run the risk of repeating the mistake the church made in Nazi Germany. The evangelical church for the most part was complacent during Israel's darkest hour. Due to a superiority attitude that was the logical result of replacement theology, it turned a deaf ear to the Jews. During this ugly period of history, what had happened to Jesus' words "Blessed are those who hunger and thirst for righteousness"?

Great, Jesus is coming back! Great, Jewish people are back in the land! Great, Arabs are coming to Christ! *The real question is, "How can believers help?"* The key to opening the door to the Middle East revival is prayer. We need you to pray. Let's start with what we're up against, and then we'll cover how to pray.

What We're Up Against with Palestinians

Palestinians have one major uphill battle! This culture is riddled with Islamic fanaticism. It will be a miracle of God to see this type of leadership passed over in favor of moderate, peace-promoting leadership. It has to be done. This will allow the church's expansion to occur, and terrorist groups will be out of a job. They will be forced to move on. Can that really happen? I believe it can. The forces of God's heavenly army cannot be matched by the powers of evil. Starting now, a new chapter in Palestinian history needs to be written. Here are some of the lowlights from the last chapter.

Pastor and author John Hagee in his book *The Battle for Jerusalem* gave the following insightful views:

> Of Arafat, Ariel Sharon said, "I don't know anyone who has as much civilian Jewish blood on his hands as Arafat since the Nazis' time." The PLO holds several records of dubious distinction:
>
> - Greatest variety of targets: between 1968 and 1980, the PLO committed more than two hundred major terrorist acts in or against countries other than Israel. Their targets included forty civilian passenger planes, five passenger ships, thirty embassies, and economic targets such as fuel depots and factories.
> - The worst midair explosion: February 21, 1970. The Popular Front for the Liberation of Palestine (PFLP) blew up a Swiss airliner, killing thirty-eight passengers and nine crew members.
> - The most sustained terrorist campaign: between September 1967 and December 1980, the PLO carried out at least three hundred attacks in twenty-six countries. Total casualties: 813 killed, 1,013 injured.
> - The largest number of hostages held at one time: three hundred passengers were held hostage on four hijacked jets. The PLO demanded the release of terrorists held by Britain, Switzerland, and Germany. The plan worked.

- The largest number of people killed and wounded by a single booby-trap bomb: July 4, 1975. Fifteen Israelis were killed and eighty-seven wounded by a PLO bomb planted in Zion Square, Jerusalem.
- The wealthiest terrorist organization: although it is impossible to determine how wealthy the PLO is, in the early 1980s it was known that the PLO had an annual income of at least eight hundred million pounds sterling.[1]

This kind of terrorism has grown to become a part of the Palestinian landscape. It has been ongoing for so long that it is routine. While I was counseling as a pastor once, a woman from a particularly disturbing family life and painful past said to me, "When all you've seen your whole life is abnormal, then that becomes normal to you." How true. How descriptive of the Palestinian state of affairs. The rank-and-file Palestinian is frustrated and tired of empty promises. The Palestinians are tired of being used politically as the focal point of desperation while their leaders live in lavish homes and spend the money intended for the people.

While on my first trip into the Gaza Strip, I had the joy of staying with a wonderful Palestinian family. Their home was very modest with no hot water or other kinds of "luxuries." As we ate a very small breakfast of cucumbers, hummus, and rice, I thanked the mom of the house. She was not a believer but a very good moral woman nonetheless. After I thanked her for breakfast, she said it was her pleasure and that "President Arafat has authorized an extra pound of rice this month for Palestinian families." Her comment was meant to be a compliment to her leader. To me it wasn't. I smiled politely, but I was finished with my breakfast! How long will they stand for this meaningless game being played out with their lives? I guarantee you, the Palestinian Authority isn't stuck with rice and cucumbers for breakfast!

This existence is considered normal and will not change with a Palestinian state. Refugees will be declared "free," yet they will remain in tents. Terrorism will not cease because Israel will not be giving Hamas, Islamic Jihad, and the other terrorist groups what they want—Israel's annihilation. Living conditions and health conditions will remain the same. Endless bundles of money will be given to the leadership to distribute among the Palestinians, and it just won't make it there. I don't believe the peace treaties will work either. There may be some temporary reprieves in the parade of violence, but peace won't last. It can't. Not while Islam is being interpreted literally from the Koran. It is in most places. Why should it be any different in Israel or in the Middle East?

Islam versus the World

In *Secrets of the Koran*, Don Richardson laid out the overall Islamic strategy for world domination. Here are the general points of the plan: legal and illegal immigration of Muslims into Western nations, a "behind-the-scenes" takeover, widening Islamic influence, a multibillion dollar international mosque construction and Koran translation program, and infiltrate Christian colleges and churches to seduce Christian women.[2]

The best place to see this happening is in England and other European countries. Since the church in Western Europe has been dead for years, Islam has gained a major foothold (although in the last few years the church is showing signs of awakening in Europe). Islam is still way in front of evangelicals as far as influence is concerned. Richardson went on: "Naive Europeans who think they are showing tolerance to a mere religion are actually inviting a very potent political invader into their societies."[3] In one instance, Prince Charles was invited to join a prestigious Muslim gentlemen's club. He joined and soon learned he was expected to show support to the club by helping the Islamic men's group accomplish something. It seems the influential Muslims of Britain coveted a piece of property owned by Oxford University. Oxford was not selling until Prince Charles pressured the academic institution to give in and sell the chunk of land to the Muslims for a new Islamic studies center.

This is what we're up against, Christians. Islam is wealthy, expanding, and becoming more persuasive within Western democracies. On American university campuses it is becoming more active. Since most colleges in America are bastions of liberalism, they become a vast moral vacuum. In Berkeley, a man sued the university because he wanted to attend school naked. Yes, he won. Islam sees the crumbling of U.S. values and attempts to take advantage of that. If a man can go to school naked for four years in the name of freedom of speech, how will we ever stop Islam? Its goal is to appear harmless at first, gain acceptance, and then plant expanding roots. To Islam, American campuses are ripe for the picking. Islam has found a base of operations on the university scene. It offers an alternative in the place where right and wrong have been dismissed altogether.

In another realm, Islam has spread like wildfire in American prisons among young black men. The latest figures show that 77 percent of young black American men grow up in fatherless homes. The dad's obligation to be a role model and be the primary moral influencer in the black home is at best happening only 23 percent of the time. Many young black men end up in prison with the lack of any parameters of virtue in their lives. When they do, Islam is there waiting for them.

Charles Colson of Prison Fellowship has noticed the alarming trend of black conversions to Islam in prisons and penitentiaries. With chaos in the inner city, Islam provides a different way. Muslim clerics promise that black inmates will not be raped if they convert and become followers of Muhammad. Also, as a black pastor friend of mine once said, "When it comes to religions, young black men desire one that has plans to take over the world, rather than one that calls for 'turning the other cheek.'" How sad that Islam is being perceived as the religion of power and Christianity of weakness. Now that's deception. Islam is on the move in prisons and in black communities across America.

What We're Up Against with Jews

I can remember once someone asked Billy Graham what he thought was the most common sin worldwide. Greed? Lust? Covetousness? Dr. Graham said that the worst and most potent sin force in the world was racism. I did not hold the same view as the esteemed evangelist until I became a missionary. I have seen the effects of it on four continents. He is right. It is a pervasive force in any culture.

More than any people in history, Israel has been a victim of racism. In chapter 11 of Genesis, God decided to separate the nations. The reason he did it in the first place was because of the rank disobedience of the people. After the Flood, God specifically commanded the survivors to "be fruitful and multiply and fill the earth" (Gen. 9:1). The people didn't want to fill the earth. They wanted to stay right where they were. They liked it there. So the Tower of Babel became their symbol of spiritual rebellion. The Mesopotamian ziggurat became a massive idol to self. The first skyscraper was built in an effort to get to heaven and have a showdown with God. Babylon, in present-day Iraq, is the location of the group's rebellious act. God put an end to it quickly. The area of Babylon has been a breeding ground for evil ever since.

In Genesis 12, God called Abram out of this culture fraught with iniquity. He told him to take a journey and didn't tell him where he was going. No exact coordinates were given, but Abram left and followed God anyway. What a contrast between

Abram and the people of Babel. The people of Babel were told to leave, and they didn't, even though God had created the nations in their midst. Abram was told to leave, and he did without knowing where he was going. The contrast between Abram as the forefather of the Hebrews and the Babylonian gang is clear. God drew Abram away from the pagan people. It became Abram versus them. Even though Abram was steeped in paganism, Yahweh pulled him out of it and took him to another region. He had His chosen people. It was God and the Hebrews against the world. It still is. Not much has changed since then. God chose the people who would later become known as Israel as His people in an eternal covenant. God chose to love them above all other peoples of the earth. Satan chose to hate them above all peoples of the earth. So it has been from the first book of the Bible until today. God and Israel against the world.

Over time the Jewish people developed a tough outer shell because of the opposition they encountered wherever they lived. A callousness has resulted—a toughness that is hard to break. If the Arab generational sin is hatred toward Jews, then the Jewish generational sin is pride. In the Old Testament, God termed this as being "stiff necked." They were proud, self-sufficient, and assumed that they had a built-in invincibility.

Let's face it—Israelis are a nation of overachievers. They excel in just about everything they put their minds to. With their God-given prosperity from generation to generation, they are often quick to remind everyone of this. Don't get me wrong—they are some of the hardest workers I have ever seen, but they have taken a certain pride in their achievements also. When I first arrived in the Holy Land, our guide told us what the difference was between American mothers and Jewish mothers. When a child goes to school in America, his mom says, "Don't forget your lunch." When a child goes to school in Israel, his mom says, "Don't forget your books." By the way, the moms on our trip agreed that he was right. So, therefore, with five major wars in fifty-five years under their belts, continual terrorism, and hostility all around them, many Israelis believe they merely have outsmarted everyone. If they fail to see the powerful hand of God sustaining them, there is only one other option. Take credit for it. Their sheer will to survive is intense. Since they are surrounded by Muslims everywhere they must always maintain a national sense of alert. They are under constant threat. People turn on them quickly. As Europe is being infiltrated with Muslims, the distance between Israel and European nations is widening. As the current intifada enters its fourth year, a European boycott has hurt Israel's already sagging economy. But they will survive and flourish again.

Some of the bravado that is normally on display in Israel is fading. This situation shows no signs of letting up. It also shows no signs of real hope on the horizon. This has hit the average Jewish person living in the land of Israel awfully hard. Some have even begun to talk about the death of Zionism. Despair is plentiful.

With the intifada continuing to take innocent Israeli lives regularly, many consider a new proposal as the answer—a wall. As Israel entered the land of milk and honey, the walls came tumbling down around Jericho. Today, they're going back up; a barrier has been built around this volatile Palestinian city. But again, the answer is flawed; it has opened up another new set of problems.

Recently on the Trans-Israel Highway, an eight-meter-high wall was built around the green line in order to keep Israeli citizens safe and terrorists out. The *Watchman's Prayer Letter* details yet another sad story for an Israeli family: "The fact that the much touted eight-meter-high wall that is being built along the green line could not save seven-year-old Noam Leibowitz is a tragedy that should have been foreseen. As the family was driving in their car on the Trans-Israel Highway, terrorists got to the Israeli side of the wall by going through the water system (draining ditch under the wall). A few bursts from a Kalashnikov rifle penetrated the car killing the one child, and injuring her sister and grandfather. The gunmen got through the drainage pipe by cutting through steel grating inside the tunnel; then they returned the same way. The failure of the wall should say something loud and clear to everyone, and it is simply this: 'Horses and chariots, only the God of Israel can save His people.'"[4] How defeating all of this must be to the average Jewish man or woman who has sacrificed so much to answer the call deep within their nature to return and reside within their homeland. Another security measure. Another way around it.

That is precisely the point. No amount of man-made devices can stop the hatred of the human heart. Racism runs deep in the Middle East soul. It has been the cultural driving force ever since God chose Abram and renamed him Abraham. Satan has seen to it. Israel is neck-deep in a swirling cesspool of racism. It is satanically inspired, and it is spreading. And Israelis cannot "think" their way out of this one. Only the God of Israel can fix this one.

The word *Hamas* is synonymous with everything that is wrong in Israel. Less than ten years ago, Hamas was a splinter group considered incapable of accomplishing anything more than occasional random acts of violence. Today it is the top threat within the borders of Israel. In recent days Egypt, the grandfather figure of Islam, has negotiated with Hamas in order to achieve a cease-fire. Abdul Ranusi, a movement leader, remarked that "cease-fire" was not in the Hamas vocabulary. The former "club" has become a movement, and its ranks are swelling. Every single peace proposal that Israel signs promises that the benefit to them will be a reduction in terrorism. They all sound similar—same song, second verse. It never pans out. It never quite materializes. Instead, terrorism groups are getting what they demand and then are expected to go away quietly. More than ever, terrorist groups are feeling empowered, and their growth is exponential.

Ariel Sharon has wiped out buildings that produce bombs for Muslim kamikazes. He has waged a war on Hamas, Islamic Jihad, Al-Aksa Martyr's Brigade, and others. Israel has unleashed modern technology to root out terrorists, and its results have ended up offending a majority of the world. One Palestinian friend from Gaza told me how Israeli Defense Forces soldiers find a terrorist in the midst of the 1.5 million people in the Gaza Strip. It seems when they locate a Palestinian willing to be an informant, they pay him maybe $250 to take a bottle of liquid and spray the top of a terrorist's car or home if possible. The spray contains strong infrared chemicals. At night, the soldiers fly over in a helicopter and perform the precision missile strike on the car or house they spot with their infrared glasses that the crew wears onboard the chopper. We have been in Gaza during the strikes. The Israeli Defense Forces usually get their man.

Herein lies the problem. There is an unlimited supply of Palestinian men and women willing to die for the cause. Israel will be shooting missiles at infrared marked cars for years. Hamas and other terrorist groups are growing faster than the Israelis can kill them.

Israel also fights tremendous battles from within. In June of 2003, Jerusalem held its second annual gay parade through the streets of Jerusalem. Since Israel is very secular, things like this are becoming normal. The nation has become a carbon copy of American culture. One year ago, the gay-pride organization tried to host its first event within the old city walls of Jerusalem. Its goal was to walk through the city gates and announce their presence in the Holy City. With strong opposition from the ultra-Orthodox and Orthodox Jews plus messianics, the parade was diverted to the more secular downtown area.

The ultra-Orthodox of Jerusalem, called Mea Shearim, segregate themselves from society. The community in West Jerusalem is strident in keeping the laws of the *Tanach* or Old

Testament. Sabbath violations are considered one of the greatest offenses. This is the place where driving a car through the community on the Sabbath will result in your car being pelted with rocks. So on one hand, a gay parade tries to enter into the old city and have free expression at Israel's holiest sites. On the other hand, the ultra-Orthodox have built their community to resemble an Eastern European Jewish ghetto that vigorously keeps the law. The diversity of the country has shattered the unity Jews experienced in the early years of their national existence. Politically, there are about twenty parties now. The country has just about everything America has as far as racial problems. With immigration streaming in from Russia, Ethiopia, and even America, ethnic tension is often high. Within Judaism, Jews from Europe known as Ashkenazics notoriously struggle with Sephardics from Spain and Arab countries and vice versa.

Are you getting the picture? It is not only a few in the land who fear that Zionism is experiencing an implosion.

The Prayer Force

That's where we come in. Every Christian needs to be a praying Christian. If you're like me, this spiritual essential needs work in your life. It does in mine. What has given me new motivation, though, has been traveling to the Middle East. Walking the streets of Jerusalem. Visiting the refugee camps in Gaza. Feeling the desperation. That is critical for prayer. We know this about Christians and prayer—we will pray if we're desperate enough. Desperation combined with faith is powerful in the life of any believer. Because people—Arabs and Jews—are now open to the gospel, now is the time to pray. Here is how you can help.

Ticker-Tape Prayers

On September 11, 2001, America was hit by an Islamic death squad. Since the situation was so fluid, and several things were developing in several locations, massive amounts of information needed to get to the American public at once. Announcers did not have time to read every story, so the solution was the ticker tape. CNN, FOX, MSNBC, and other stations began using a running recap band on the bottom of the screen. It kept the public abreast of the changing situation and condensed the lead news stories of the day. The first time I remember seeing it was when our president was being flown around the country to safety. I remember being angry that the networks might actually be exposing his whereabouts. If terrorists could get CNN, they might be able to track the commander in chief and other leaders. Of course, the White House was in a declared state of war, and to protect our president, reports deliberately listed several places he might have been.

George W. Bush was God's man to guide America through the worst national tragedy our country has ever undergone. He stood tall. As a believer, he also sought the face of God for help in the midst of the chaos. It was evident the power that resonated from our president was a result of God working in him and from all the prayer that was directed toward heaven on his behalf. According to the World Prayer Center in Colorado Springs, our president now has an official prayer team of well more than two million intercessors. This is the official list, yet perhaps millions more pray for him daily. Since then, the prayer team for the president and the ticker tape have stayed. Here's how we can combine them both.

The ticker tape is a built-in emergency prayer alert for Christians. It is something that we can utilize on a daily basis as an up-to-date prayer mobilizer. If you're like me and you overdose on news, you have to guard against two things:

1. Avoid becoming a fear-based Christian. The news is depressing! If you're not careful, it will wrap you up in overwhelming anxiety. In Israel, many Palestinians and Jews don't watch the news. I asked a Jewish woman in Jerusalem why no one seemed to watch the news in Israel. She said, "It's because the news makes us go crazy!" Good point! If you exist on a steady stream of news and fail to take "every thought captive to the obedience of Christ" as Paul told us to in 2 Corinthians 10:5b, you'll probably struggle with cynicism or depression. Wait a minute, Christian; we win this thing in the end, remember?

2. Make the news a spiritual experience—make it a time to pray. I'm serious. The ticker tape highlights the hottest spots of conflict worldwide. The latest stories from spiritual warfare front lines are the majority of the unrest and evil from around the globe. The two are connected. Here's an example. The war in Iraq was really an effort to keep an Islamically controlled state that had designs on Israel and had an emerging and advanced weapons program under control. True there are many other things involved, yet at the core is fundamental Islam that has its sights set on Israel and the West.

    Also, it did help that Saddam Hussein believed he was Nebuchadnezzar in a reincarnated state. Nebuchadnezzar was the only Arab leader to ever defeat Israel and control their land. In 586 BC, the Babylonian captivity removed the Jews from their beloved land and returned them to the place Abram started from. God wanted the nation to start over, and he took them back to their roots in Mesopotamia. True, Nebuchadnezzar did defeat Israel, but only because God let him. Of course, this is overlooked. In

Jeremiah 34:2, Yahweh told the prophet Jeremiah what was coming: "I am about to hand this city over to the king of Babylon, and he will burn it down."

Amazingly, an event that occurred in 722 BC became added motivation for Saddam's preparation to strike Israel. The conflict was motivated by religion. As far as the Middle East goes, that is usually the root of the problem.

Praying with the Ticker Tape

Seeing Gaza in the news is a regular occurrence. Let that set off an alarm in you to pray! There is one evangelical church in the Gaza Strip. One! When you see the latest border clash with Israel, try not to get sidetracked—prayer is what is needed. The church of dynamic believers in the Gaza Strip needs your fervent intercession.

Jerusalem, Tel Aviv, the West Bank, Haifa, Galilee, Gaza—all of these places have a vibrant church that has the extremely difficult task of doing ministry within the war. They are strategic placements of the church within the spiritual war zone. They need your prayers daily.

Throughout the Middle East in radical Islamic pockets, there is a vibrant church present and serving Jesus with united hearts. Did you know there are brothers and sisters in Saudi Arabia and an underground church in Mecca? When you see a story on Saudi oil, terrorism, or the Muslim annual pilgrimage called the *hajj*, pray for the church there. It is illegal to be a Christian in Mecca, Saudi Arabia. Christians are killed there. The house church movement needs your prayers.

In Tel Aviv, the messianic congregations need your continual prayers. The congregations need prayers in Jerusalem. When you see Jewish cities or settlements in the news on the ticker tape, let it be like a *shofar* blowing to beckon the chosen people to a biblical feast. It is a call to prayer. These Christians are doing front-line ministry. They are at the bomb blasts. They are attending funerals. They are trying to bring the light of Jesus Christ into the darkness. They need spiritual reinforcements. They get tired and frustrated as we do. Prayer is what keeps them going.

In a recent bus blast, an American believer who lives in Jerusalem was on the bus and miraculously survived. He was dazed and wandered home. His family gave praises to God that he lived, and then they were horrified to find pieces of flesh all over his back from the deadly explosion. This is life in the land of the Bible these days. No one should have to live like this. Prayer is their lifeblood. We must lift them up in prayer.

After working with ten Iraqi churches in Jordan, I fell in love with these outgoing, joy-filled believers. Do they ever know how to worship God! It was before the "Gulf War" of 2003, and we were welcomed with open arms. After spending the day with them, we tearfully said good-bye. The leader of the retreat said, "I have a message for the American people. Tell them that Iraqis are praying for them!" How humbling! The Iraqis praying for us? Considering what they were facing, we should have been on our faces daily for them.

God has sufficiently chastised me and my wife, JoAnn, in the need for prayer. Especially for Israel and in the Middle East.

Internet Prayers

Several Internet sites can keep you updated on the latest needs of the church worldwide. If you want your prayers to go global, get on the Net:

DAWN (Discipling a Whole Nation) is a Christian research and strategy ministry. It has an excellent resource called the Friday Fax that updates prayer needs weekly. (www.dawn ministries.org)

World Prayer Center, an Internet interactive prayer site, is a great place to pray for current needs globally. You can even listen to praise music as you have your own personal prayer session. (www.prayerteam.org)

The Voice of the Martyrs is dedicated to the persecuted church. This is one of my favorites. It will connect you to believers and their needs from hot spots of persecution worldwide. (www.persecution.com)

CFI (Christian Friends of Israel) offers *Watchman's Prayer Letter*, a monthly report e-mailed directly to your computer. CFI has a heart for Israel and will keep you updated on the latest from Israel. (www.CFIJerusalem.org)

Mission Network News is a daily report of five to six top stories from around the globe. Some of the stories give the results of what God is doing in a particular area. Some stories give breaking prayer needs. This is another good prayer site. (www.gospelcom.net)

AD 2000 and Beyond's "Praying through the Window" program states, "The core of the unreached people of our world live in a rectangular-shaped window. Often called 'the Resistant Belt,' the window extends from West Africa to East Asia, from ten degrees north to forty degrees north of the equator."[5] This AD 2000 ministry coordinates all kinds of prayer initiatives. This is also one of the best sites. (www.ad2000.org)

EvangeCube has a good and practical Web site. You can link up with what God is doing around the world. We have an updated prayer list from front-line churches and a way you can equip your church to share Christ with the EvangeCube. (www.evangecube.org)

There you go. Seven ways to turn your computer into a weapon of prayer. The Internet has much evil connected to it, but we can use it as a powerful tool for God to mobilize large prayer groups. Get connected.

"With every prayer and request, pray at all times in the Spirit, and stay alert in this, with all perseverance and intercession for all the saints" (Eph. 6:18).

Thirty-One-Day
Prayer Journey through Israel

A good way to use this for devotions is to read a Proverb, then pray for the corresponding city of the day. The cities are listed below, and a prayer map at the end of the photos section will help you locate each day's prayer site.

Day	Place	Day	Place
1	Jerusalem	17	Caesarea
2	East Jerusalem	18	Tulkaram
3	Tel Aviv	19	Netanya
4	Nablus	20	Palestinian Refugee Camps
5	Haifa	21	Eilat
6	Jenin	22	Latrun
7	Tiberias	23	Hadera
8	Ramallah	24	Jewish Kibbutzim
9	Nazareth	25	Safed
10	Jericho	26	Acco
11	Joppa	27	Kiryat Shmona
12	Bethlehem	28	Afula
13	Ashkelon	29	Ashdod
14	Hebron	30	Israeli Government Offices
15	Beersheba	31	Palestinian Authority
16	The Gaza Strip		Leadership

Pray for gospel exposure and conversions, churches to grow and plant new churches, biblical reconciliation between Jews and Arabs, revival to spread to the rest of the Middle East, and all mission groups in the area, such as the International Mission Board, Campus Crusade, Youth With a Mission, EvangeCube, and Global Missions Fellowship.

Travel to Israel

This is the best way to pray—on location. Every year prayer groups travel to Israel. They tour biblical sites and help local churches and ministries. But above all, they pray. This is done through many ministry groups. As believers saturate the area and the people with passionate prayers, Satan's strongholds will begin to loosen, and salvation will occur. This is an exciting way to immerse yourself in God's work in Israel.

Today, many people are afraid to go to Israel; yet Jews and Palestinians need us more than ever. In fifty-five years, only a handful of American tourists have been killed. As Christians, we must advance the gospel into the dark parts of the world without fear. Muslims are sending missionaries to America. Are we going to sit back and do nothing? We have the words of life. We have the solution to all the hate. We have the power of the Spirit of God within us. We have the promise that Jesus will build His church. Why not take a trip to the front lines where the action is?

People ask all the time, "Aren't you afraid to go to Israel?" I believe in the sovereignty of God and that He alone has our days numbered. Of course, we are not to test the Lord and do something stupid. We don't live on the dangerous edge for some twisted thrill. Yet we are to take the gospel everywhere. My good friend Curtis Hail once said, "Until it is my time to go and be with Jesus, I am bulletproof." So are you!

In conclusion, global praying that is truly biblical is needed above all in Israel and in the Middle East. Passionate prayer. Prayers of faith. Continual prayer. Fasting. Weeping before the Lord. All of these are needed. Both Jews and Palestinians are desperate. Will we share that desperation with them? We must.

Prayer is number one. We must advance on our knees first. Chapter 9 will tell you what else you can do.

Chapter 9

Waking Up the Western Church

The vast resources God has lavished on us from heaven are needed to spread the gospel, disciple new believers, and plant strong churches in the Middle East. It's time for action and strategic involvement in the biblical heartland. Every believer should help and can; here's how.

The Responsibility of the Blessed

I am guilty. I have sinned greatly against my country America. It happens every time I return home from a mission trip. I get critical of America. I try not to, but inevitably it happens. When seeing the unmet needs of the rest of the world, it's hard not to compare it to our abundance. We have so much. God has blessed America like no other nation throughout history. This is the generation that has it all. In the past few years, the United States has undergone a recession. With corporate scandals and a sagging stock market, Americans have been worried about the future. "What about my 401(k) plan?" "Will I have enough for retirement?" "Will I be able to provide for my children in the days ahead?" All of these questions are important ones. Scripture is clear about financial planning. The point is that we are privileged to be able to ask those kinds of questions. How many people around the world don't ask these questions because they have no possibility of ever attaining those things? The answer, of course, is the majority of the world.

Is blessing bad? No. Those are gifts from God's gracious hand. James reminds us that "all good gifts" come from heaven. They are ours to enjoy. Most importantly, they are ours to use. Our resources can make a major difference for the cause of Christ globally. We will give an account one day at the judgment seat of Christ for everything. The gifts that the Holy Spirit bestowed on us at His discretion will be examined. Did we use them for God? If we were given the gift of encouragement, who was encouraged? If the Spirit of God gave you the gift of evangelism, was anyone saved as a result of it?

Our resources will be examined also. Time to get the checkbook out, folks! Did we spend it all on ourselves? Could we have made a difference for Jesus with all of our stuff? Did we waste it on the superficial that burns in the end anyway? What survived the fire and transferred into eternity? Kingdom results are what we're looking for. We are responsible.

Another question we could be asked is, "How did you treat God's chosen people?" The church in history has a notoriously bad history with Jews. If nations are judged for it, what about the church?

The church needs to be Israel's best friend. We must. Before we look at how we can do it, let's take a quick review of Israel's history for the last twenty centuries.

Whatever Happened to the Jewish Race?

The New Testament church began about AD 30 (read Acts 2). God still had an unconditional covenant with the Jews. We often lose perspective of this as we become absorbed in our own Christian history recorded in Acts 2 through the rest of the New Testament and on to today. What did happen to Israel after the church began? Get up to speed with this condensed time line:

AD 30	Jesus' death and resurrection. The church is born.
66–73	First Jewish revolt against Rome.
70	Second Jewish temple destroyed under Roman General Titus and tenth Roman Legion fulfilling Jesus' prophecy in Matthew 24:1–2. A majority of Jews scatter.
132–35	Second Jewish revolt against Rome called the Bar Kokhba Rebellion—1.5 million Jews killed; 985 villages and 50 fortresses destroyed in Israel.
136	Roman Emperor Hadrian renames Jerusalem Aelia Capitolina and builds pagan temple over site of temple. Jews banished from Jerusalem.
222–35	Roman Emperor Alexander Severus allows Jews to begin visiting Jerusalem again.
306	Christian church Council of Elvira forbids marriage to Jews and bans all relationships with Jews.
415	Cyril, bishop of Alexandria, encourages violence against the city's Jews. He incites Greece to kill or expel Jews.
571	Muhammad, the founder of Islam, is born.
627	The Arabian holocaust begins. Muhammad kills thousands of Jews in Medina and surrounding villages. He takes Jewish women and children as slaves.
637	Muslims capture Caesarea and force Jews to wear yellow patches for identification.
692	Dome of the Rock built on first and second temple site by Caliph Abd el-Malik.
722	Leo III of Constantinople forces Jews to "convert" to Christianity.
1096	First Crusade. Jews massacred in European cities.
1099	Crusaders capture Jerusalem and massacre thousands of Jews.
1227–74	Thomas Aquinas, a well-known church theologian, calls for all Jews to become slaves.
1229	King Henry III of England forces all Jews to pay half the value of their property in taxes and orders Jewish worship be conducted quietly so Christians do not have to hear it while passing by synagogues.
1267	Vienna city council forces Jews to wear cone-shaped hats and badges to identify themselves.
1285	In Munich, Germans burn 180 Jews alive in city synagogue.
1321	Jews accused of poisoning France's water wells. More than 5,000 Jews killed before King Philip admits they were innocent.
1348–49	Black death (bubonic plague) blamed on Jews; 210 Jewish communities destroyed in Europe as retaliation.
1391	Archbishop Ferrand Martinez of Spain campaigns against Jews and kills 10,000.
1420	All Jews expelled from Lyon, France.
1493	Jews expelled from Spain; 200,000 leave.
1496	Portugal expels Jews.
1516	Jewish ghettos begin in Venice.
1537–41	Suleiman the Magnificent, ruler of the Turkish Ottoman Empire, rebuilds Jerusalem city walls with seven gates and Tower of David that all stand today.
1543	Martin Luther writes About the Jews and Their Lies, an anti-Semitic booklet. He uses the term "vermin" for Jews.
1555	Pope Paul IV builds Jewish ghetto in Rome and forbids Jews from owning real estate. They are forced to wear caps to identify themselves.
1615	King Louis XIII of France gives Jews one month to leave or face death.
1622–29	Persian Jews are forced to convert to Islam.

1648	Over 100,000 Jews massacred in Poland.	
1670	Jews expelled from Vienna.	
1730	First synagogue built in America in Manhattan.	
1781	Joseph II of Austria drops "badge law" for Jews after 513 years.	
1834	The Spanish Inquisition ends.	
1840	"To Jew" becomes a verb to describe unethical business practices.	
1860	Theodore Herzl, the father of modern Zionism, is born.	
1862	Gen. Ulysses S. Grant expels all Jews from Kentucky, Tennessee, and Mississippi.	
1866	Jews become the official majority in Jerusalem again.	
1879	Nobel Prize winner Albert Einstein born.	
1886	David Ben-Gurion, Israel's first prime minister, born.	
1896	Herzl publishes *The Jewish State.* Zionism is born.	
1903	British government proposes a home for Jews in Uganda.	
1916	Ottoman Empire of 400 years collapses. Turks no longer rule Middle East.	
1917	Russian Revolution claims 200,000 Jewish lives.	
1921	Jordan established, taking land promised to Jews for the new Israel.	
1922	Balfour Declaration of Great Britain promises future home for Jews in Eretz Israel (the land of Israel).	
1925	Hebrew University opens on Mount Scopus, Jerusalem.	
1930	British white paper stops Jewish immigration to Israel.	
1932	Saudi Arabia is established. Iraq gains independence from Great Britain.	
1933	Adolf Hitler becomes chancellor of Germany. Cardinal Pacelli, who becomes Pope Pius XII, issues Hitler Concordat and accepts Nazi	

socialism and anti-Semitism as core values.

1938 Kristallnacht—Germany burns down Jewish synagogues. Charles E. Coughlin, American Catholic priest, launches media campaign against Jews. Catholic churches display Nazi flags and ring their church bells to welcome Nazi troops in Austria. Nazis begin forcing Jews to wear yellow stars to identify themselves. This is copied from the church.

1939 S.S. *St. Louis* carrying more than 900 passengers is turned away from America and Cuba.

1942 Nazi leaders adopt Final Solution for Jews at Wannsee Conference.

1943 King Christian of Denmark stays in his Nazi-occupied country and helps 7,000 Danish Jews escape death camps. To empathize with Jewish families marked by the Magen David, the king, even though Christian, wears one himself.

1945 WWII ends and Nazism falls. Holocaust, which claimed 6 million Jewish lives, ends.

1947 U.N. proposes Jewish state. Dead Sea Scrolls found in Qumran.

1948 Israel becomes a nation, May 14, 1948. British mandate ends May 14, 1948. Five Arab armies invade Israel May 14, 1948. President Harry S. Truman recognizes the state of Israel in its first hour of existence.

1948–49 Israel's War of Independence.
1956 Suez War.
1967 Six-Day War. Israeli Air Force attacks Egyptian, Jordanian, and Syrian air bases and defeats Arab armies.

1968	PLO calls for Israel's destruction.
1968–70	War of attrition with Egypt.
1973	Yom Kippur War with Egypt and Syria.
1975	U.N. equates Zionism with racism.
1981	Israeli Air Force destroys Iraq's nuclear reactor that threatens Israel's national survival.
1982	War in Lebanon.
1987	The Palestinian intifada (uprising) begins in Israel.
1991	The Gulf War begins. Israel attacked with Iraqi Scud missiles. Arafat backs Saddam Hussein.
1993	Oslo Agreement between Prime Minister Rabin and Chairman Arafat is signed.
1994	Yitzak Rabin, Yasser Arafat, and Shimon Peres are awarded Nobel Peace Prize.
1995	Rabin is assassinated. King Hussein begins Dome of the Rock restoration.
1998	Israel has its 50th birthday. Hamas pledges to renew the intifada if Jerusalem is not the capital of a Palestinian state by 1999.
2000	Israel withdraws from Lebanon. Intifada begins again. Prime Minister Ehud Barak offers the Temple Mount to Arafat for peace. He turns it down.
2003	Operation Iraqi Freedom in Iraq. "Road Map for Peace" adopted by U.S., calling for a Palestinian state within three years.

No wonder historians estimate that the Jewish race should have grown to be 120 to 130 million by now. The Jews number approximately 12 million people today. Yahweh's chosen people have endured a sustained assault since their very beginning. Satan has inspired a variety of people groups to become Jew-haters throughout time.

"A thief comes only to steal and to kill and to destroy" (John 10:10).

However, in God's millennial kingdom, when He rules the earth, all opposition to the Jews will be silenced. Even Israel's longtime enemies will turn to God and give up their hatred.

On that day there will be a highway from Egypt to Assyria. Assyria will go to Egypt, Egypt to Assyria, and Egypt will worship with Assyria. On that day Israel will form a triple [alliance] with Egypt and Assyria—a blessing within the land. The LORD of Hosts will bless them, saying, "Blessed be Egypt My people, Assyria My handiwork, and Israel My inheritance." (Isa. 19:23–25)

Jacob will no longer be ashamed and his face will
no longer be pale. For when he sees his children, the
work of My hands within his [nation], they will honor
My name, they will honor the Holy One of Jacob and
stand in awe of the God of Israel. (Isa. 29:22b–23)

This will be quite a quantum leap for Israel. The Jews will
go from being the despised of the world to the favored of all. A
critical event will happen for Israel before all of this takes
place. They will repent and discover their Messiah. They will be
cleansed. "On that day a fountain will be opened for the house
of David and for the residents of Jerusalem, [to wash away] sin
and impurity" (Zech. 13:1).

What a glorious turnaround for Israel! Finally, Jews will be
revered and honored. They will no longer have a host of enemies trying to wipe them out. That will all be over. When Jesus
rules from Jerusalem, they will be safe. Jerusalem will live up
to its name—it will be the "city of peace."

Do we Christians have any input into this? Will the God of
Israel use us to help restore them to Him? Will we have any
influence in their eternal destiny? I believe so. I also believe
that because of our Judeo-Christian roots in America, we have
stayed on course in our overall support of Israel. America is the
one place where the church has stood strong for Israel for the
most part. As Bible-believing Christians, we may not always
have had the purest motives. We may have been more excited
that the end times appeared closer since the Jews are back in
the land. We may also have been morally convicted about their
ongoing persecution. Now it's time to empathize with them.

Maximizing the Moment

Jewish people ought to feel that Christians are there for
them no matter what. They ought to be able to sense our love
and respect for them. The *Voice of the Martyrs* says that

Christians are being persecuted in fifty-five nations. Almost one-fourth of the world hates the church and wants its progress slowed or stopped altogether. Globally, Jews and Christians are the two groups of people most often persecuted and killed. The fifty-five nations that violently oppose us are for the most part Muslim. Communism is still a foe too. Yet, isn't it interesting that since September 11, 2001, Jews and Christians realize they have a common enemy—fundamental Islam. We should have realized this earlier. Plainly, it is in the Koran, according to former Islamic professor Mark Gabriel:

> "Take not the Jews and the Christians as auleya (friends), they are but auleya of each other. And if any amongst you takes them (as auleya), then surely he is one of them." (Surah 5:51)[1]

> "O you who have been given the scripture (Jews and Christians)! Believe in what we have revealed (to Muhammad) confirming what is (already) with you, before we efface faces (by making them like the back of necks; without nose, mouth, eyes) and turn them hindwards, or curse them as we cursed the Sabbath-breakers. And the commandment of Allah is always executed." (Surah 4:47)[2]

If a Muslim reads the Koran literally, he will not want to be a friend of Jews or Christians. Not only that, he has koranic justification to kill them. Now, as I have said before, for the majority of Muslims a literal rendering of verses such as these is untenable. They see *surahs* like these as outdated and no longer applicable. To them, this is merely history that was fulfilled at the beginning of Islam. The wars that helped establish it as the "power religion" of the day are now over and done with. The majority of Muslims have not made it their personal life goal to fulfill these verses and kill Jews and Christians. They may not especially like us, but murder is out of the question.

Yet there are Muslims who wholeheartedly support the literalness of koranic interpretation. Every *surah* to them is binding for today and must be realized for Muhammad's followers. In the eighteenth century, a movement within Islam started an effort to move Muslims back to this kind of literal interpretation. The Wahhabi branch of Islam grew over time. Saudi Arabia finally embraced it, and it became the underpinning of the House of Saud. Since 1932 when Saudi Arabia became a nation, the Wahhabi belief has driven the Saudis to a stricter, more traditional form of Islam. Hence, that's where the majority of the September 11 terrorists were from. Their belief system took them to the logical end—to kill Christians. The fact that we support Israel made it even more appealing.

After September 11, our common enemy was identified. Jews are being killed by strict Muslims. Christians are being killed by strict Muslims. There are 109 verses in the Koran on war. This does not include verses in which war is mentioned in a story. These are the verses that command or encourage war. Muhammad himself fought in forty-seven wars. This problem is not going away very soon, folks.

There is also another group on the Islamic "hit list." It is Arab believers—whether they be Palestinians or Jordanians or Iraqis. They are in a frightening situation that controls their lives and their existence. The believers in Gaza live in it. That's why they have given their lives to share Christ's love within the world of Islam. It is their only hope to change anything. Gabriel wrote, "The leader of Libya, Muammar Qaddafi, considers himself to be a great thinker, and he announced one day that he had a solution to the problem. His solution was for the Christians to convert to Islam, and then they would be brothers and sisters with the Muslims, and the fighting would stop. Qaddafi said, 'I hope there is a new generation of Lebanese Christians who will wake up one day and realize Arabs cannot be Christians and Christians cannot be Arabs, so then they will convert to Islam and be true Arabs.'"[3]

The lines are drawn in the sand—Christians, Jews, and Arab believers versus the world of Islam. Over 1.3 billion Muslims are now spread out globally. If the fanatics are only 10 percent of Islam, that still is a major force. One hundred thirty million is roughly half the size of America. Fanatics could have lower numbers or higher.

Here's how to maximize the moment:

Love a Jewish Person

In America, Jewish people are approachable and often open to relationships with believers. If we seek them out and really befriend them, it will be a great start.

Ask for Forgiveness

I know we had nothing to do with the anti-Semitism of the Roman Catholic Church during the Middle Ages. Certainly what happened in the Spanish Inquisition repulses us. Nazi German treatment of Jews and the Holocaust were even worse. How could the black death be blamed on the house of David? But these events did happen in supposedly Christian countries. How will Jewish people know that we detest those "false works" of our Christian faith unless we tell them? Look at some of the things that Christian leaders had to say about Jews. Martin Luther, Augustine, Origen, and Chrysostom all had strong anti-Semitic feelings. They also were in places of leadership, and thus they helped direct the Christian masses toward anti-Semitism.

After you have established a loving relationship with a Jewish person or even a family, next, hit the problem head-on. Here's what might be appropriate to say: "You know, with you being Jewish and me being a Christian, we both have a lot in common. We believe in and read the same prophets. We believe the God of Israel will be the victor at the end of time. But as a Christian, I want you to know that I am aware of how the church at times has been at the forefront of Jewish persecution. It was wrong, and I ask your forgiveness. I was ignorant about the dark side of Christian history until recently, and I repent before you. Please forgive us. I believe Christians ought to be the best friends Jewish people ever have. I want you to know I will never be a part of anti-Semitism. If I see Christians who have even a trace of this, I will correct them. You have my word."

Encourage Jews

Wow, how's that for an icebreaker? We believers are children of the truth. We bring the good, the bad, and the ugly into the light. When we do something like that, real spiritual healing can take place. I love the words of Isaiah when prophesying about the coming Redeemer. He said the Messiah was going "to comfort all who mourn, to provide for those who mourn in Zion; to give them a crown of beauty instead of ashes, festive oil instead of mourning, and splendid clothes instead of despair" (61:2b–3a). Jesus' very presence brought the Jews honor, joy, and hope. As His followers, let's do the same for them today.

An Israeli government official in the Netanyahu administration named David Bar-Illan once said this to our church tour group: "Look, we Jews have so few friends in the world that we'll take them where we find them!" Doesn't that sound like people who need believers to put their arms around them and love them?

Do you know about the Steven Spielberg project? After he directed the movie *Schindler's List*, Spielberg decided to film the testimony of every remaining Holocaust survivor worldwide. Quite an ambitious goal. He has labored on this project for years now. Since many survivors are older and passing away, Spielberg tried to do the personal interviews as quickly as possible. Once a person dies, if he has no remaining relatives, his story will be lost forever. One problem Spielberg encountered was surprising. It seems that the *Shoah* (Hebrew for Holocaust) had left some survivors in so much pain and fear that they did not want to tell their stories. Many of them feared that they might suffer recriminations if they told what really happened. What depth of pain the Jews have endured!

They need us. They need our friendship, need our love, our support, our understanding. Their pain is enormous. Church of Jesus, let's be the home base of Jewish blessing. Stan Kellner, a good friend of mine, is a believer and he is Jewish. Stan has shared the gospel with his people for about twenty-five years. Here are some practical pointers from this experienced veteran of Jewish outreach:

- Not every Jew is an Old Testament scholar.
- Not every Jew is observant. Define scriptural terms for Jews, such as *sin, salvation,* and *eternal life.*
- Portions of church history have contributed to "gentilizing" the church. Help your Jewish friends understand that they are made complete in the Messiah.
- Use Scripture with your Jewish friends. God's Word will always make an impact on them.

Share with Sensitivity

The last thing we believers need to do is try to coerce a Jewish person with a tract containing the four spiritual laws. They don't need us to rush them. Listen to their objections. There are reasons why they haven't received Jesus as their Messiah. These reasons usually are not based on the person of Jesus but rather on the character of His followers. Here are three important hurdles for Jewish people:

1. "If I become a Christian, then I'm no longer Jewish."

   Answer: Becoming a Christian has nothing to do with being a Gentile and forsaking your Jewishness. It is all about a Jewish person embracing the Jewish Messiah, however.

2. "How do I know if Jesus fulfilled the Bible's prophecies of the Messiah?"

   Answer: A good question and of utmost importance to a Jew. If you are unfamiliar with the prophecies, here are a couple of great chapters loaded with future promises that Jesus fulfilled: Psalm 22, Christ on the cross, and Isaiah 53, the explanation of the cross.

   Also, Jesus can be traced all the way through the Psalms. Here are a few prophetical verses in the Psalter and the corresponding verses in the New Testament indicating the prophecies' fulfillment:

Psalm	New Testament	
2:7	Hebrews 1:5–6	The Messiah would be the Son of God.
16:8–10	Luke 24:5–7	He would be resurrected from the dead.
22:1–21	Matthew 26–27	He would agonize on the cross.
34:20	John 19:36–37	His bones would not be broken.
41:9	Luke 22:48	A close friend would betray Him and reject Him thoroughly.
68:18	Ephesians 4:8–10	He would ascend to heaven.
69:21	Matthew 27:48	He would be offered vinegar on the cross.
89:3–4	Luke 1:31–33	He would be a descendant of David.
96:13	1 Thessalonians 1:10	He would return to judge the world.
110:1	Matthew 24:44	He would be the son of David, yet David's Lord.
118:22	1 Peter 2:7–8	He would be rejected by many people but not by God.

This is all good, solid evidence for a seeking Jewish person. In chapter 7, Jewish commentaries were quoted from trusted rabbinical writings. These can be helpful too. What's important is to make the discussion into some kind of a spiritual showdown. When a Jewish person asks a question, answer it with a question as Jesus often did. If the question is, "How do I know if Jesus fulfills the Bible's prophecies of the Messiah?" a good question/answer would be, "What do you think about these Scriptures?" Invite the person to read over the verses on his or her own and get back together later.

3. "What will my family think?"

Answer: (Truthfulness is extremely important here.) If your family is the typical Jewish one, they probably won't like it at all. Remember, Jesus said this is a probability. He also said, "The person who loves father or mother more than Me is not worthy of Me" (Matt. 10:37a).

Those are tough words, for sure. But in many cases, God uses the child to reach his parents and gently lead them to the Savior.

Let's Review

1. Start a friendship with a Jewish person and honor that person as Jesus did.
2. Ask forgiveness for past church sins. Assure the person of your friendship and commitment to stand with him and against anti-Semitism in the future.
3. Encourage her by appreciating her spiritual heritage.
4. Share with sensitivity. Look for common ground.
5. Answer his questions. He has good reasons for them. Scripture given to them to read on their own can be a powerful tool. Ask the Holy Spirit to illuminate the Word of Yahweh and open his heart to these words in a new way.
6. At the proper time give her a chance to receive Yeshua as her personal Savior. When the Holy Spirit convicts her, she will be ready. I have seen this over and over.

Love a Muslim

The majority of Muslims are God fearing, zealous, committed, and humble and don't hate Americans. I feel as comfortable in the West Bank or the Gaza Strip as I do in Jerusalem. I love these people, and I want you to love them also. Believers, these people are open to Jesus. We cannot let this moment pass without swift action. But before we talk strategy, let's take a crash course in Islam. Don McCurry is an expert on the subject and has labored in Muslim outreach for more than forty years. His booklet *Now You Can Know What Muslims Believe: A Muslim World Overview* is an excellent primer on Islam. Here are some background essentials to help you deal with Muslims:

MUSLIM BELIEFS AND PRACTICES—From Muhammad's teaching and life, a double-edged movement was born: the religious and the political. (Islam makes no distinction between the two.) Religiously, the essence of Islam can be broken into two categories: the beliefs (Iman) and the duties (Din). In reality, there are hundreds of items in the area of beliefs and thousands in the area of practices; but for practical purposes, they are summarized under six articles in each category. These are the distinctives of Islam.

The Belief System of Islam (Iman)

1. There is one God. He has no partners (no Trinity). He does not beget (like humans; therefore, God could not have a Son). He is absolutely sovereign, responsible for all that happens (thus making Him the author of evil).

2. God created angels. These angels are everywhere. One sits on one's right shoulder recording one's good deeds; another sits on one's left shoulder recording the bad deeds. On judgment day these records are opened and on the basis of them the person is rewarded or punished. Satan was formerly an angel. He was turned into a jinn because he disobeyed God in refusing to worship Adam. Jinn are another order of supernatural beings, supposedly created from fire. They can possess humans.

3. God appointed prophets for every age. This line starts with Adam, includes many biblical characters, such as Noah, Abraham, Ishmael, Isaac, Jacob, Joseph, and others like David, Solomon, Jonah, Zechariah (the father of John the Baptist), John the Baptist, Jesus, then a couple of nonbiblical prophets from Arabia, and finally, Muhammad. In this schema, Jesus is only a prophet, and Muhammad is the last and greatest of the prophets, the "Seal of the Prophets."

4. Holy Books. Every prophet was given a Holy Book by God. Supposedly there were as many as 124,000 prophets from Adam to Muhammad. Muslims believe that all of these holy books have been lost except the *Torah* (Law) given to Moses, the *Zabur* (Psalms) given to David, the *Injil* (Gospel) given to Jesus, and of course, the Quran, *or* Koran (Recitation) given to Muhammad. Muhammad believed each book was preexistent and was sent down to each prophet as needed. Muslims believe the same thing today.

5. The Day of Judgment. God will judge the world on the "Day of Doom." Everyone's good deeds will be weighed in a balance scale against his bad deeds. A wonderful sensuous paradise of gardens, fruit trees, streams, rivers of wine, and black-eyed virgins will be awarded to every man whose good deeds outweigh his bad deeds. A fiery hell is the reward of those whose bad deeds outweigh their good deeds.

6. The Decrees of God. Everything is determined by a Sovereign God. He is responsible for everything, including evil. He chooses to lead astray whom He will and to guide aright whom He will. No one can withstand His decree on any point.

THE DUTIES OF ISLAM (Din)

1. The Confession of the Creed (Shahadah): "There is no God but God and Muhammad is the Messenger of God." To say this and mean it makes you a Muslim. If you renounce this faith after once you have made this profession, you are to be put to death.

2. Ritual Prayer (Salat). The good Muslim is to say his prayers five times a day: (1) just before day-break, (2) at noontime, (3) in mid-afternoon, (4) at sunset, and (5) anytime after sunset before going to sleep. This has to be done in Arabic exactly the way Muhammad did it and taught it.

3. Giving of Alms (Zakat). Giving one fortieth of your income to the poor or religious causes is mandatory. Voluntary giving *(Sadaqat)* is also encouraged.

4. Keeping the Thirty-Day Fast (Sawm). This is done during the lunar month of Ramadan. It comes eleven days earlier every year. It is not a complete fast. You may not eat from just before daybreak until sunset every day. You may eat as much as you want between sunset and sunrise. You are supposed to study the Quran, *or* Koran, during this month, reading one thirtieth each night.

5. Going on the Pilgrimage (Hajj). This is oblig-atory, once in a lifetime for all healthy people who

can afford it. The pilgrim is to go to Mecca, walk
around the "House of God" (the Kaaba) seven times,
stone the devil, say his prayers at the "Station of
Abraham," drink water from the well of Zamzam (in
memory of Hagar and Ishmael), and several other
things.

6. *The Duty of Striving in the Way of God
(Jihad, Holy War)*. A few Muslims, especially in the
West, try to say that this is not a duty. But the Quran
or Koran teaches it, Muhammad practiced it, and
Muslims have practiced it ever since.

The overall goal of Islam is to conquer the world
by any means necessary: war, preaching, economic
inducement or coercion. Since their religion is the
"right" religion, and Muhammad was the "last and
greatest Prophet" and he taught it, every Muslim is
obligated to participate until Islam is the religion of
everyone on earth.[4]

OK, now that you are familiar with the basic beliefs and
duties of the religion, let's go on. How do you love a Muslim?

Confess Your Prejudice

One problem we Westerners have with Muslims is that we
often stereotype them. I know this from experience. I did it.
After I had been to Israel for the first time, I was so Jewish-
focused that I wouldn't give Muslims the time of day. I shared
the bad news throughout this book about radical Islam. Now as
you prepare for outreach, remember most Muslims are very
nice, warm people. The chances are slim that they have a bomb
under their jacket. They probably don't work for Hamas. They
do need Jesus, however. They will listen to you. If they are traditional and dress like seventh-century Arabs, don't let that
throw you. Ask God to give you a love for Muslims. He can give

you a passion to reach them. He will tenderize your heart for them. They are about 21 percent of the world's population. Your effort and participation in this world outreach program is vital.

At this point, I must confess the prejudice I had toward not only Muslims but Arabs at one time. Again, my love for Israel seemed to overshadow the needs of the Arab people. I was not driven to them especially. I felt in some way that if I reached out to Arabs or Muslims I was forsaking Israel. But you know what? God's love is for all people. Both Jew and Arab. He wants Ishmael's descendants saved too. I have learned that you can love Israel. You can honor Jews and support them and still love Arabs too. That's OK with God. Just because I believe Israel has a biblical and historical right to their land doesn't mean I can't also have a desire to reach Arabs with Jesus.

I was in a Denver restaurant years ago, and two Arab men walked in. They both had black leather coats on and spoke with heavy Arab accents. All of this Middle East stuff was new to me, and I immediately began to judge them in my mind. *I bet they're terrorists. Maybe they've been planted in America as spies.* (Lots of other real edifying thoughts like those.) Well, wouldn't you know that the two men came and sat right next to me at another table. I began to kind of eavesdrop like Maxwell Smart or Inspector Clouseau. I felt I surely would uncover a sinister plot already underway.

I did learn a lot about them by listening to their conversation. To my horror, I soon realized that these two men were believers! I began to hear them talk about what the Lord was doing here and what the Lord was doing there. Did I ever feel like two cents! *What a jerk you are, Tom! You judged them just because of their race.* Those thoughts ran through my mind. Then it got worse. I said hello and said, "Are you guys believers?" They said, "Yes, we're believers from Syria. Are you one too?" At that point I felt so bad I doubted I was a believer myself! I reluctantly said, "Yes, I am." Immediately these brothers told me all about their mission trips into Syria and how dangerous it was for them to share the gospel at home. They also worked in orphanages there. They invited me to go with them next time. Man, I was feeling worse by the minute! I had judged them. They sure didn't judge me though. Before I knew it, one of the brothers insisted that I follow him home for coffee and to meet his wife and kids. I went. I had a blast. There is nothing like Arabic hospitality! These people were like long-lost relatives.

I went to missionary training school that afternoon. I learned that as Americans we often carry prejudice toward Arabs and Muslims in general. Get rid of it or you'll go through life and never reach one of them.

Begin a Friendship

In America there are Muslims in most major cities. The population is growing, and America has about equal numbers of Muslims and Jews. They enjoy religious freedom here, and that is new to them if they're from the Middle East. Muslims, when they migrate West, tend to leave some of their tradition behind. Often women and men drop the robes and burqas prevalent in Islam-controlled areas. If they do keep their traditional clothes, they probably are somewhat isolated in the United States. They are used to this and often crave friendships. After September 11, Muslims encountered much misunderstanding in our country and underwent much public scrutiny. Muslims in traditional garb especially felt the stares of wondering people in public places.

My wife and I were shopping in a Denver department store, and the woman who waited on us was Arab. Her accent had a familiar tone. I asked, "Are you from the Middle East by any chance?" She said, "Why do you ask?" I replied, "I travel there quite a bit, and I love Arab culture. I love the people, the food, and their warmth. I was just curious." Sensing I was accepting of her, she then answered, "I'm from Iraq, but I don't like to tell people that." I said, "I bet that's hard at times for you. I hope you feel welcome in America." She said, "Thank you very much!" This is typical I think. She wasn't dressed in traditional Muslim clothes, but as we visited awhile, I could tell that she was fairly open. She was approachable, also, after she realized that I appreciated her culture.

Get to know a family. You'll be surprised. Once you've been in their home and been blessed by their hospitality, you'll have friends for life. We must build bridges with Muslims if we expect to reach them for life.

Ask Questions

Muslims love to tell people about their religion. They hope to "set us straight" and often talk freely about their faith. Dedicated to their religion, they fail to see the huge spiritual gaps that exist within Islam. They are works motivated. They pray five times a day. They read the Koran.

Yet the great spiritual chasm for Muslims is in the area of atonement. Who will pay for their sins? What sacrifice will satisfy God? What happens to their sins? Muslims have no answer to those questions. With their theology of works justification, they have no certainty that they will ever make it to paradise. When it comes to terrorist acts, this is often the motivation behind the violence. The rationale for these crimes is usually to win enough points with Allah to earn salvation. In places where women have become suicide bombers like in Israel, the motivation is usually to erase a serious offense. Women who are divorced bring disgrace to their family, and this is seen as a quick fix to restore honor.

Muslims struggle with the very same thing that all God-fearing people who don't know Christ struggle with. The question they cannot answer is whether they will have enough good works to outweigh the bad works. Will they be on the positive side of the ledger when they die? Will they build up enough equity in life to earn a place in eternity? Of course, we can show that ultimately that system breaks down, since even one sin unpaid for would exile us from heaven forever.

So after you develop a solid friendship, investigate a little. Nonthreatening questions that are asked gently and not aimed at starting an argument can make them think about things. Here's one: "As Christians, we believe Jesus paid for our sins because we are incapable of doing it ourselves. What do you as a Muslim believe?"

Since Muslims believe Jesus was a prophet, ask what your friend thinks of him. How about this question: "As a Muslim, have you ever wondered what Jesus was all about?" And later, "I would like to tell you about Him. Would you tell me about Muhammad?"

If you ask penetrating questions in a spirit of love, the relationship will continue even if he is not ready to trust Christ as his Savior. Always remember, do not be condescending; do not argue.

Power Praying

If we Christians will love Muslims and build friendships with them, the doors will fling wide open for the saving power of Christ. After we have a spiritual dialogue in a calm and affirming atmosphere, the next step is most important. Get on your knees. If we pray for the Muslims that we know every day, we would start to see results. God has given the church in America a golden opportunity. Muslims live throughout our country. We can do a lot to erase their notions about Christians in general. Most of all, the Holy Spirit will use the relationship. He will begin to penetrate Muslim souls with your love and concern.

Pray with them also. Muslims usually react positively when you ask them if you can pray for them. Who doesn't need prayer? "Do you have anything I can be praying about for you?" We have tried this in refugee camps in the Gaza Strip with Muslims. They often keep their eyes open because they are curious about Christians who pray with passion. The fruit of the Spirit in our lives is so attractive to them!

Believer, you have power in Christ. Put it to work. Reach out to Muslims. The fields are ripe. Now that's a way to engage in missions right here in the United States. You can get involved with Israel and the Middle East.

Get Global

If you've been a Christian for years and you find yourself getting complacent, you probably need to be mission challenged. It's easy being a Christian in America. We don't suffer persecution, and we have every kind of Christian resource available for our use. We have more churches than ever in America. Sadly, though, our general church numbers have been stagnant for the last twenty years. We are not growing as we should be. Why is this? I believe it's because we're not persecuted. We don't have a real possibility of going to jail for being a follower of Jesus Christ. Therefore, we lack a sense of desperation. Since we're not desperate, it affects our prayer lives. Our prayer lives affect everything else. If we're not desperate in our prayers and grappling with God over lost souls, our prayers become shallow and often self-centered. If I don't feel especially moved that my next door neighbor is going to die one day and go to hell, then the bulk of my prayers probably will be filled with "gimmies." "God, I need this." "Can I please have Your help with this one?" In other words, I become totally self-absorbed.

But, believer, God expects more from you. Much more. You are a part of the single, biggest rescue project in the history of mankind. God's power is moving across the globe today. Salvations are up—way up. I know we're not seeing it here in America, but trust me, it's happening. That's why it's imperative to get globally connected. If you plug into what God is doing in the world today, you'll not only be able to help believers around the globe, you'll be more intent on it happening in America. Use the Web sites mentioned in chapter 8 to get started.

In a pastors meeting in Colorado Springs a few years ago, the participants talked about what makes an effective church. A diverse group of Christians—Southern Baptists, Presbyterians, charismatics, and others—the preachers represented churches that were vibrant and growing. Also, they had at least one other thing in common: a heart for the world. God blesses churches and believers who long for Him to reach this world with His glorious gospel.

Is your church snoozing through the current revival? Here are four ways your church can wake up.

1. Get your pastor on a mission trip. Believe me, he will have the time of his life. There are plenty of great mission groups to go with. EvangeCube and Global Missions Fellowship offer 100 to 150 mission campaigns a year. I personally lead at least five per year to Israel and the Middle East. You can get in touch with us at www.evangecube.org. If your pastor can go only once a year, your church will change. Mine did. I say this from experience since I was the senior pastor who was coaxed to go by people within the church. On my first mission trip, I led more people to Christ in one week than I did in one year back home! That will charge up any pastor.

2. Pray fervently. Start a prayer group in your local church. You can do this in a home Bible study or in an adult Bible fellowship class. Use chapter 8 for resources, or if you have a group of missionaries that

your church supports, pray for them. Prayer letters are revitalizing to your foreign missionary family. They often feel forgotten on the field. These are heroes of our faith. Your communication will bless them.

3. Give generously. After you support your local church, why not give to the churches outside of America? Their resources are so little that often they have nothing or very little coming in financially. Giving to the work of God in the Gaza Strip, Jerusalem, or Amman, Jordan, for example, is a great investment. These believers make the most of every day and will be faithful with your gifts.

   If your church is excited about missions, maybe you can adopt a church, a city, or a region. Right now, ministries are looking for that throughout Israel, Jordan, and Egypt. U.S. churches should give a minimum of 10 percent of their income to missions. Encourage your pastor to begin moving your church's percentage of giving upward toward 20 percent.

4. Maximize your possessions. There is no doubt that God has blessed us in the United States. We should not be ashamed of it in any way, but rather be thankful. God is going to hold us believers accountable for how we use our resources. Here is the test to see if all your possessions mean too much to you, to determine if they are controlling you. Would you be willing to give them all away? (Would I?) If God said, "I want you to move to Israel and reach Jews and Arabs for My sake," would you do it?

Maybe God is calling you to downsize. My wife and I are in the process of doing just that. It's tough with six children, but we know this is what God wants for us now. Pay off those credit cards, and even if you sent a portion of that to the front lines, it would make a huge difference.

Catch the Wave

I believe, in America, we are experiencing the second wave of missions. Initially, as God raised up America, we fulfilled a strategic role that no other country could have. We were and are today, without a doubt, the primary force behind world evangelization. We in America send more people, more money, and more resources to the mission field than any other nation. We are privileged to do so. The majority of mission agencies are from the United States. The world's two largest mission organizations are American. Campus Crusade and Southern Baptists have thousands of missionaries in the field each year.

During world evangelization, something happened along the way with the American church. It peaked and its growth began to slow considerably. I know many churches in the United States are reaching the lost and in the midst of their own growth spurt. But overall, the outreach of U.S. churches has been flat for two decades now.

I believe that we now need to learn from the church in the mission field. They have only a fraction of what we have in America as far as opportunities for training, resources, and funding. Yet they are more effective than we are.

That's where the wave comes in. The first wave went out from America, and its evangelistic splash covered the world. Now churches in the mission field are sending a wave back toward us in the United States. Their zeal and simplicity is pointing us American believers back to our spiritual roots. A much simpler church is where I believe we're headed in the West. Prayer, fasting, evangelism, discipleship, Bible study, and the spiritual disciplines are all major components of the mission field church. Those basics are what American churches need today. We must aim at excellence, yet stay true to the essentials of our faith. We don't have to aim at sophistication. We do have to be passionate about everything we do for Christ though. That's what we can learn from churches in other parts of the world.

They are effective, unpretentious, focused, and have a great amount of passion. Desperation combined with all-out passion is powerful. Bring these characteristics back to America in our day, we pray, O Lord!

Two Nations under God

Why should America care about Israel? Because we have often been the sole friend of the nation of Israel. God has lavished rich blessings on our country as a result of our honoring His people, Israel. His promise to bless those who bless Israel and to curse those who curse Israel still affects the destiny of nations today. America is no different and will pay a very high price if we ever turn our backs on Israel. It will be our greatest national disaster.

Judaic, Christian, and Islamic roots run centuries deep in Israel and even more so in Jerusalem, the spiritual capital of the world. Religion, politics, culture, and history have all had a head-on collision in the Holy City of God. The four of these disciplines individually or corporately have no chance of solving the region's conflict. They just don't have the right solutions to defuse the powder keg that is already lit. Since the problems are spiritual in essence, sorting out the Middle East maze demands spiritual answers if anything is to be resolved. Satan is using radical Islam to stir up as much Jewish resistance as he can worldwide. In Exodus 34:24, the God of Israel promised, "For I will drive out nations before you and enlarge your territory. No one will covet your land when you go up three times a year to appear before the LORD your God." Israel enjoyed life in the land for a time. Amazingly, there were three land components given to the nation of Israel. Satan is desperately trying to undo all three of them today.

Exodus 34:24	*Today*
I will drive out the nations from the land.	Nations are now trying to drive Israel out of the land.
I will enlarge your territory.	Israel's territory is now shrinking.
No one will covet your land.	The entire world covets the land of Israel.

The answer to the Middle East puzzle is Jesus and His church. Israel needs to turn to her Savior. The church should be Israel's best friend. Scripture promises that Israel will one day repent and embrace Jesus as Messiah. We can and should be the people who help move the Jews in that direction. The church is called to influence Israel.

Because we support Israel does not mean Palestinians are out in the cold. The church is the answer to their problems also. Radical Islam will not deliver what it promises to the Palestinian people. It will continue to make guarantees that it has no capacity to make good on. Palestinians need to dump their leadership that is driven by fanatical Islamic dreams—such as the destruction of Israel.

We must support the awesome Palestinian believers who are making a major impact in the world of Islam. They are power-houses for God. Palestinian believers and messianic believers are experiencing true reconciliation in the midst of the volatile land of Israel. Jesus and His church are proving to be the only answer to the centuries of war and conflict. God's love is for all people. Palestinians desperately need to be assured of the American church's support too.

The moment to maximize our impact is now. The mission heart of God is bringing about a revival in Israel and in the Middle East. You are needed for strategic intercession. God is using the growing intensive prayer movement focused on Israel and also the Middle East. As followers of Jesus in the Western church, our involvement is the biblical heartland. In doing so, God also wants to wake up the church in the United States. He wants both Israel and America to have a vibrant church today. It is the real hope of both nations, America and Israel, who are called to be two nations under God.

Acknowledgments

Thank you to the following people for their vital contributions to *Two Nations under God*. To:

Mom and Dad Doyle for all of your unconditional love, support, prayers, and encouragement along the way.

Mom Renda for loving me like a son and for your help with research.

The Doyle, Renda, Crispell, Bell, and Merritt families because of your continual love and encouragement.

Ginger Bromley for your joyful attitude and lightning-fast typing.

Curtis Hail for your friendship, leadership of Global Partners, and vision to reach the world for Christ.

Nathan Sheets for your friendship and passion to reach the lost through the EvangeCube that God graciously gave us through you.

Jeff Sheets for your friendship, business expertise, creativity, and ability to make me laugh.

Casey See for your friendship and being the steady rock of EvangeCube.

The EvangeCube team that lives to serve and that I am honored to work with: Helen, Nancy, Julia, Lisa, Jennifer, Carey, Jim, Steve, Mike, Ted, David, Luke, Melanie, Retta, Lindsay, and Joseph.

The EvangeCube Board of Directors that keeps us steady and motivated at the same time.

Allen Reedall for covering me and my family in prayer.

Barbie Kolar for being the "Indiana Jane" of the Middle East.

Peter Pintus for modeling biblical leadership.

Lorraine Pintus for your expert coaching.

Charlie Dyer for your love for Israel that spilled over to me.

Doug Cecil for being persistent in getting me to Israel.

Mike and Cheri Fitzsimmons for sharing dreams with us.

Dianne Passno for believing in this project and introducing me to the wonderful people of Broadman & Holman.

The Broadman & Holman team of Gary Terashita, David Shepherd, John Thompson, Lisa Parnell, Greg Pope, and Marc Whitaker. All of you have been such a blessing! You are not only talented, and godly, but a blast to work with.

Our support team and prayer team. Thank you for investing in God's great work in the Middle East.

Our home group of Don and Debbie Boatwright, Darnell and Leslie Boehm, Waynerd and Ginger Bromley, Paul and Tami Engel, Paul and Connie Lundeen, and Mitch and Frances Sikich. Thank you for loving us and sharing our excitement for God's work in Israel and the Middle East.

We love you all! Tom and JoAnn Doyle

Special thanks for the great pictures to:

Tom Kirk	Eric Axley
Kit Kirk	Paula Axley
Barbie Kolar	Peter Pintus
Allen Reedall	Rob Van Dusen
Jay Straub	

Notes

Chapter 1: Extreme Spirituality

1. Charles L. Feinberg, *Israel at the Center of History and Revelation* (Portland, Ore.: Multnomah, 1964), 78.

2. Ehud Avriel, *Open the Gates! A Personal Story of "Illegal" Immigration to Israel* (New York: Atheneum, 1975), vi.

Chapter 2: Endangered Species

1. F. F. Bruce, *Israel and the Nations* (Downers Grove, Ill.: InterVarsity, 1997), introduction.

2. Ibid.

3. H. Wayne House, *Israel the Land and the People* (Grand Rapids, Mich.: Kregel, 1998), 27.

4. Ibid., 28.

5. Avriel, *Open the Gates!*, 190.

6. Feinberg, *Israel at the Center*, 135.

Chapter 3: A Promise That Shaped America

1. "United States Literature," *Encyclopedia Judaica*, vol. 15 (Jerusalem: Kregel, 1971), 1571.

2. Ibid.

3. Ibid.

4. Ibid.

5. Ibid., s.v. "United States of America; Anti-Semitism, 1654.

6. Joshua Brandt, "Voices from Doomed *St. Louis* Haunt Researcher," *Jewish Bulletin of Northern California* (Oct. 8, 1999).

7. John Cornwell, *Hitler's Pope: The Secret History of Pius XII* (New York: Penguin, 1999), 80.

8. Erwin W. Lutzer, *Hitler's Cross* (Chicago: Moody, 1995), 102.

9. Ibid., 146.

10. Ibid., 147–48.

11. Ibid.

12. Ibid.

13. Larry Collins and Dominique Lapierre, *O Jerusalem* (New York: Simon and Schuster, 1972), 28.

14. Ibid., 27.

Chapter 4: Dangerous Alliances

1. Tim Dowley, *Eerdman's Handbook to the History of Christianity* (Grand Rapids, Mich.: Eerdmans, 1977), 269–70.

2. Amotz Asa-El, *Spectacular Israel*, ed. Shai Ginott (Hugh Lauter Levin Associates, 1998), 14.

3. Mark Gabriel, *Islam and Terrorism* (Lake Mary, Fla.: Charisma House, 2002), 81–82.

4. David Dolan, *Israel in Crisis* (Grand Rapids, Mich.: Revell, 2001), 94.

5. "Arab Antisemitism Documentation Project," Middle East Media Research Institute (May 2003), Special Dispatch Series No. 446.

6. Mark Gabriel, *Islam and the Jews: The Unfinished Battle* (Lake Mary, Fla.: Charisma House, 2003), 92.

7. Dolan, *Israel in Crisis*, 96–97.

8. Don McCurry, *Now You Can Know What Muslims Believe: A Muslim World Overview* (Colorado Springs, Colo.: Ministries to Muslims, 2001), 15.

Chapter 5: Heroes of Our Faith

1. Benjamin R. Barber, *Jihad vs. McWorld: How Globalism and Tribalism Are Reshaping the World* (Great Britain: Corgi Books, 2003), xxvii.

2. Ibid., xxvviii.

3. "Why a Magazine? Why Kivun?", *Kivun*, ed. Tsvi Sadan (June 2003), 2.

4. Brother Andrew, *The Calling* (Nashville, Tenn.: Moorings, 1996), 224.

Chapter 6: The Believer—The American

1. Randall Price, *In Search of Temple Treasures* (Eugene, Ore.: Harvest House, 1994), 77.

2. "U.S. Warns of Sanctions against Israel," iafrica.com, August 6, 2003.

3. *The Jerusalem Post*, Special Supplement (February 21, 2003), 2.

4. *Voice of the Martyrs* (Bartlesville, Okla., May 2003), 6–7.

5. Ibid.

6. Ibid.

7. Baruch Maoz, "A Faithful Witness in Israel," *Banner of Truth* (Carlisle, Pa.: Banner of Truth), June 21, 2003.

Chapter 7: The Mission Heart of God

1. Hussein Sumaida with Carole Jerome, *Circle of Fear: My Life as an Israeli and Iraqi Spy* (London and Washington, D.C.: Brassey's, 1991), 40.

2. Steve Herzog, *Jewish Culture and Customs* (Bellmawr, N.J.: Friends of Israel Gospel Ministry, 1997), 57.

3. House, *Israel the Land and the People*, 274.

4. Thomas Cahill, *The Gift of the Jews: How a Tribe of Desert Nomads Changed the Way Everyone Thinks and Feels* (New York: Anchor Books, 1998), 3–4.

5. John Hagee, *Final Dawn over Jerusalem* (Nashville, Tenn.: Thomas Nelson, 1998), 58–60.

6. David Dolan, *Israel at the Crossroads* (Grand Rapids, Mich.: Revell, 1991), 34–35.

7. Theodore R. W. Lunt, *The Story of Islam* (London Church Missionary Society, 1909), 36.

8. Abd El Schafi, "Behind the Veil" (Colorado Springs, Colo.: Voice of Truth Press, 1996), 77–124.

9. Don McCurry, *Healing the Broken Family of Abraham* (Colorado Springs, Colo.: Ministries to Muslims, 2001), 277–79.

10. Ibid., 177–78.

Chapter 8: Global Praying That Is Truly Biblical

1. John Hagee, *The Battle for Jerusalem* (Nashville, Tenn.: Thomas Nelson, 2001), 55–56.

2. Don Richardson, *Secrets of the Koran* (Ventura, Calif.: Regal Books, 2003), 162–74.

3. Ibid., 170.

4. Lonnie C. Mings, "Hamas Road Map to Violence," *Watchman's Prayer Letter* (July 2003), 1.

5. AD 2000 and Beyond, www.ad2000.org, October 1999.

Chapter 9: Waking Up the Western Church

1. Gabriel, *Islam and Terrorism*, 35.

2. Ibid., 35–36.

3. Ibid., 83–84.

4. McCurry, *Now You Can Know What Muslims Believe*, 2–4.